The Diner's Guide to Wines

The Diner's Guide to Wines

HOWARD HILLMAN

HAWTHORN BOOKS, INC.
Publishers/NEW YORK
A Howard & Wyndham Company

To a nameless wine drinker who, several thousand years ago, was the first to discover that certain wines go better with certain foods, and to the untold number of wine lovers who have added to this field of knowledge—and therefore our pleasure—by discovering new wine-food affinities.

Contents

II

Other Tips and Insights

III
Encyclopedia of Foods
and International Dishes

IV
Mini-Guide to Wines

Index

Introduction

Wine-food affinities are taken too seriously by some people, while too lightly by others.

Belonging to the first group are the pseudogourmets, those epicurean illiterates who, pontificating, forecast culinary doom if—God forbid—you don't make the ideal match-up between a wine and food. The truth of the matter is that once you learn the basic easy-to-grasp affinity rules summarized in Part I, it is unlikely that your wine-food pairings will be objectionable.

The second group, the culinary anarchists, believe that the pursuit of wine-food affinity is, in a word, hogwash. This opinion not only runs counter to centuries-old experience but also to modern scientific knowledge. Certain wines do improve the flavor of certain foods, a result of natural chemical reactions, among other factors.

What I am trying to point out is that while a mismatch is unlikely to cause you any undue displeasure (and therefore you shouldn't be overly concerned about that eventuality), a properly matched wine and food will significantly increase your pleasure—a positive and worthwhile goal.

To illustrate this approach that seeks to increase gratification rather than to avoid an unlikely displeasure, let's suppose we have selected a crisp French *Grand Cru* Chablis of good vintage to drink with a glazed Smithfield ham. There is little doubt that we will derive some satisfaction from the Chablis and ham—both are too good not to enjoy, even when consumed together. At the same time we haven't really made the best possible choice because the Chablis is too subtle and dry to stand up to and fully harmonize with the ham's heavy sugar and salt content. There are far better alternatives, as this book will show.

Wine also serves other pleasure-producing functions at a meal. It is enjoyed for its own sake, it relaxes the diner and creates within him a warm inner feeling of self-content, and it stimulates camaraderie, wit, and philosophic discussions. Glasses of wine glistening in candlelight can also help transform an ordinary occasion into one of romance and/or elegance.

Wine performs another vital service of which few people are aware. It helps relieve sensory fatigue. Your taste and smell receptors quickly become desensitized to outside stimuli, whether these flavors and aromas are agreeable or unpleasant. Here lies one reason why the first sample of a dish is often the one that is enjoyed the most. To fight sensory fatigue you have two primary options. You can give your papillae and olfactory receptors a half-hour rest in between bites—obviously not too practical. Or you can refresh those glands by tasting and smelling a different, yet compatible, substance such as wine (other items like a nibble from a piece of bread or from a plate of lightly seasoned baby peas or a sip of water also work, but not usually quite so well as wine and certain other relatively mild alcoholic beverages, such as a fine lager beer or ale). Using this palate-refreshing method, you prolong the heightened enjoyment of your entrée, whether it be a roast leg of lamb or a broiled Maine lobster.

Getting more for your shopping dollars is a very practical by-product of mastering wine-food affinities. Let us take the case of the previously cited example of serving a French *Grand Cru* Chablis with a glazed Smithfield ham. The primary reason that a *Grand Cru* Chablis costs a few dollars more than an ordinary French Chablis is that the first has delicate and refined qualities that are more sought after than the second wine. Those extra dollars will be more or less wasted if you do go ahead and drink the *Grand Cru* Chablis because, as was pointed out before, the ham's sugar and salt content will render your palate incapable of detecting the extra subtleties that you have paid for in your *Grand Cru.* You would have been just as well off if you had served the non-*Cru* French Chablis (and even better off, as you'll learn later, if you didn't serve a Chablis in the first place). Over a period of a year or two, a few dollars saved here and there could add up sufficiently to get you a case of Château Lafite-Rothschild, or whatever your favorite great wine may be.

I
Wine Selection Factors

Practically every diner knows this catchall rule of thumb:

Red wine with red meat,
White wine with white meat,
Rosé or Champagne with everything.

I wish it were that easy. Unfortunately, that set of guidelines is far too general to be of any practical use to a discerning diner, as too many exceptions to the rule exist. For instance, a light red rather than a white wine is usually more compatible with a roast chicken, a white meat.

Further confusing this already complicated situation is that wine selection involves a myriad of variables that must be considered in conjunction with each other.

But take heart because this section summarizes these complex variables for you in a logical, organized manner, enabling you to select a near-perfect, if not *the* perfect, wine to accompany a particular dish or meal.

Enemies of Wine

Wine, like most entities in life, has a number of natural enemies, and you must be cognizant of them if you wish to treat good wines with the respect due them. For the benefit of quick reference, I have drawn up a "least wanted" list of the foods that seem to be the biggest culprits as far as day-to-day dining habits are concerned. For the specific details on how each of these foods affect wine, consult the appropriate entry in Part III, the encyclopedia portion of this book.

- Artichokes
- Asparagus
- Bananas
- Candied vegetables (carrots, yams, etc.)
- Chocolate
- Citrus juices (orange, grapefruit, lemon, etc.)
- Coffee and, to a much lesser degree, tea
- Cranberries
- Egg yolks
- Hot spices and pungent condiments (chili, curry, Worcestershire sauce, Tabasco sauce, mustard, horseradish sauce, etc.)
- Molasses
- Oily fish products (canned tuna, anchovies, sardines, pickled herring, etc.)
- Onion family (especially garlic)
- Pickles
- Pineapples
- Sugar and other sweet substances (hostile to dryish wines)
- Tomatoes
- Vinegar (wine's worst enemy)

It is important to keep the damaging effect of each of these enemies in proper perspective. Some, like vinegar and chocolate, can be vicious villains, while others, such as artichokes and asparagus, are not quite so hostile. The quantity (and to some extent, the quality) of the villainous ingredient you consume is a factor, too. A touch of vinegar in a sauce, to cite an example, will probably do minimal damage to your taste buds. Contrary to the opinion of some people, you can even reduce the potentially negative effects of a vinaigrette salad dressing. Simply cleanse your palate with a piece of bread or other neutral food prior to taking a sip of the wine. Another ameliorating factor is the credentials of the wine you are trying to protect; if it is an ordinary rather than a fine wine, it has fewer subtle qualities worth protecting, and consequently, you need live in less fear of having your wine ruined by the various enemies.

The best way to become familiar with the potentially harmful effects of these enemies is to conduct some simple experiments in your own home. Here's how: While your palate is fresh, take a sip of wine, then eat a sample of one of the enemies (bananas, for instance), then retaste the wine. You should be able to notice a change in the taste and a marked decline in the virtues of the wine, particularly if the wine is a good one.

When conducting your experiments, you might also want to investigate how certain ingredients are an enemy of one type of wine but are on friendly, or at least neutral, terms with another wine. Fish is a good example. While it is always in conflict with a strong, full-bodied, heavily tannic red wine, fish can at times be pleasantly combined with an unassertive light- to medium-bodied, low-tannic red—as is the case with Matelote, a famous Burgundian fresh water fish stew that is cooked and often served with the latter type of wine.

Enemies other than food exist, too. Tobacco smoke, the most prevalent offender, can blunt the smoker's palate. You're in trouble even if you don't indulge in cigarettes, cigars, or pipes because the secondhand smoke wafted your way, courtesy of your neighbor, can lower the sensitivity of your palate and olfactory receptors. Some taste experts go so far as to consider secondhand smoke more harmful to the senses than the firsthand variety.

Another nonfood enemy is the common cold and its respiratory cousins. Few things in life are a greater waste than serving a fine wine to a person suffering from a cold, hay fever, bronchial asthma, or a similar malady. You can easily prove this point to yourself by experimenting the next time you fall under the curse of one of these afflictions. Your first sniff and sip should provide conclusive evidence.

Time-Tested Affinities

On the other side of the coin, wine has its best friends, as we shall soon discover in this subsection on the classic wine-food affinities.

These well-accepted affinities didn't come about because some epicure or venerable gourmet society arbitrarily decided that a certain wine was the ideal accompaniment for a given dish. The roots of the traditional match-ups are at least a century old and sometimes thousands of years old, the result of trial and error. Most of these affinity rules have met the challenges of each succeeding generation's critical wine drinkers. Whenever one of these new generations discovered that an apparently iron-clad rule was really only an assumption that had turned into dogma, it deleted the fallacious rule, which in turn further refined the body of knowledge on wine-food affinities passed down to the next generation.

Over the past quarter century, at least one major change in the wine-food affinity rules has been evolving. While today's educated diner still realizes that there are many wrong wines for a particular dish, he now recognizes that there is never a single best wine. This was not the case in the past. The majority of the very influential turn-of-the-century Parisian and London gourmets, for instance, felt that a big Côte de Nuits Burgundy was *the* wine to go with a fine roast beef, and to consider any other wine on equal terms with the Burgundy was sacrilegious. The primary reason they didn't also include on their exclusive list other equally suitable wines, such as a top-quality Italian Barolo, is that those other wines were not readily available. Today, especially in America, the large-city dweller who plans to have roast beef can usually find a worthy Barolo as well as a vast range of other superb wines at one of his quality local wine shops. Times are changing.

Of the world's many classic wine-food affinities, these are perhaps the most famous:

- Brut Champagne (or vodka) with caviar
- Red Bordeaux Médoc with "high" game
- Red Côte de Nuits Burgundy with prime roast beef
- French Sauternes with a ripe peach
- Vintage Porto with a mature Stilton cheese
- *Premier* or *Grand Cru* Chablis with plump oysters
- White Montrachet or Meursault with a delicate-flavored and fine-textured butter-sauced poached fish such as a turbot or sole
- White Swiss Neuchâtel with Fondue
- Retsina or Kokkineli with Moussaka
- A quality chilled rosé with a picnic lunch

There are also hundreds of regional classic affinities that are not shared by the whole wine-imbibing world. Many Germans love serving their quality sweetish wines with game, while a number of Bordeaux gourmets relish eating pâté de foie gras with a luscious Sauternes. In olden Bordeaux times, the Sauternes was even served with the fish course, an act that is seldom practiced today.

Some affinities are recent inventions that seem to have been created by tourist-pleasing restaurants and then quickly accepted by their patrons as gospel. Paella with Sangria is a perfect example. While both are Spanish specialties, the Sangria's excessive sugar content will do little for the Paella's delicate-flavored shellfish. Moreover, Paella comes from

Valencia and Sangria from Andalusia, two distinct culinary regions of Spain that have little in common save their shared Spanish language and national government.

One classic affinity deals in negative rather than affirmative terms: Serve the great German Trockenbeerenauslese with nothing (a summer garden and a few good friends is all you need). Sound advice.

Drinking the Wine with or without Food

Selecting a wine to go with any type of food can be misleading if we sample the wine by itself, without food. At a wine tasting, for instance, we may reject a wine because it has too much of an acid taste—but when drunk in tandem with food, this seemingly negative acid quality is a blessing. If wine tastes just right without the food, it will appear too mild and flaccid when imbibed with food.

If we are choosing a wine to be drunk by itself, such as at a cocktail party or when guests casually pop over on a Sunday afternoon, then most of our dinner wines would not be appropriate because there would be no food—or at least, not the right type of food—to foil their extra acid. A milder, softer, easier-on-the-palate wine, such as a medium-priced German Rhine wine or even a California white jug wine from a quality winery would be more suitable.

The Age, Quality, and Condition of the Cooking Ingredients

Generally speaking, the younger an ingredient is and the better its quality, the more delicately flavored it will be. Well-known examples of this rule of thumb are lamb versus mutton, small versus oversized eggplant, and freshly picked versus yesterday's corn.

The Fat Content of the Dish

As the fat in a dish increases, you should generally look for a more acidy, assertive, robust, and/or fuller bodied wine, as these qualities have a knack for cutting through fat, thereby making the dish more digestible. A wine with pétillant or sparkling characteristics can also foil a fatty dish.

Fat can be incorporated in the dish via the main or secondary cooking ingredients or through the sauce or the cooking medium, such as the oil used in frying.

The prime source of fat in a dish is usually the main cooking ingredient. This is particularly true when you are cooking the flesh of one of those naturally fatty animals such as goose, duck, pig, and sheep. Even certain fish tend to be on the fatty side: salmon and trout, to list but two. Other well-known fatty dishes include pâtés, terrines, and *confits*. Sauces can also be on the fatty side, including those butter- and cream-enriched sauces of Normandy.

How the Food Is Prepared

It would be nice if I could tell you that wine A always goes well with chicken while wine B loyally harmonizes with fish, but I can't. Besides, if I could, I would not have had to write a book of this length. While the chief cooking ingredients do indeed influence our selection of wine, there are other factors, the most important one being how we prepare our food. I am referring to the cooking method, the seasoning, the marinade, the stuffing, the garnish we select for our main cooking ingredient, be it beef, chicken, lamb, mutton, pork, fish, shellfish, game, whatever. Still another critical determinant is the sauce, a topic that is discussed in the next subsection.

The cooking method is so influential that at times it even determines whether a red as opposed to a white wine would be the most appropriate. Take the case of chicken, a relatively neutral meat for which there are scores of distinct cooking methods, not to mention a million different recipes. If we roast the chicken, a light-bodied red would probably be best, but if we stew it in a cream sauce, a full-bodied white would be more in order. Other examples of how the method of preparation influences the choice of wine are flambéeing with brandy (a fine wine would be wasted); blanching and presoaking (insufficient soaking of a Smithfield ham, for instance, would make the meat even saltier than it normally is, thereby ruining our taste buds for virtually any wine); deep frying (this cooking method usually takes a fuller bodied wine than if the food were panfried); marinating (young venison goes well with a Médoc, but if the meat is marinated, a Côte de Nuits would probably be better).

Some spices are hot or pungent and thereby palate stunners, an obvious threat to good wine. But the type of seasoning is only part of the equation. A minute pinch of cayenne in a pot will have minimal effect on our palate, while an overdose of otherwise mild parsley will fatigue our taste buds. Likewise, a light touch of vinegar in a dish is an innocent caprice, while a heavy-handed use of salt or Cognac will overwhelm our palate.

When eating assertively spiced dishes such as some of those of the southern Indian, Tex-Mex, Thai, and Szechuan cuisines, wine is almost always a poor choice. A more compatible match-up would be a beer or ale, the more character and nobility, the better. (Heineken and Kirin brands are among those that I would recommend.) If you insist upon a wine, an average-quality Gewürtztraminer would be one of your best choices.

Though not quite so palate scorching as the previously mentioned ethnic foods, many of the dishes from France's

Provence and Italy's south are infused with strong herbs, semiassertive spices, garlic, and other aromatic products of these sun-drenched lands. Wine is not only allowable, but is appropriate, so long as you stick to the robust reds and full-flavored whites, the same general type of wine that comes from those regions. Even a rosé, if not too sweet or mild, would not be wrong. What would be incorrect would be soft-spoken wines, such as a Moselle or any wine costing more than a few dollars retail.

The stuffing of a dish will significantly influence your wine selection, especially if it contains dried fruits. Because these shriveled fruits (prunes, raisins, apples, apricots, etc.) are sweet, you need to select a sweeter wine than would otherwise be required. This is the reason that I and a lot of other wine-loving cooks shy away from dried-fruit stuffings.

The garnish can or cannot matter, mainly depending on whether it will be eaten or remain purely as a visual ornament. The garnish most likely to be found is parsley with a slice or wedge of lemon. As lovers know, a nibble of parsley can be a breath freshener, but watch out for the lemon. If you have a good wine, I wouldn't suggest squeezing more than a tiny drop or two of the lemon juice onto your seafood lest the citric acid affront your beverage.

When food is marinated, the resulting dish will be incompatible with the fine wine. The reason is that if a marinade is to perform its tenderizing chores, it must contain a sufficient quantity of acid. Marinades also tend to be strongly flavored, a characteristic that is again belligerent to fine wines. Even if you used nothing but a great wine to marinate a food, you are still in trouble, because by the time the wine has done its tenderizing job, it will have become somewhat acidy. That is why it is wasteful for someone to serve a fine wine with marinated game, as is the custom in certain lands, including Germany.

The Sauce

Sauces play an important role in wine selection, sometimes to the point where your sauce has more to do with which wine you select than the main cooking ingredient, particularly if it is an ingredient like shellfish, fish, chicken, pork, or veal. The flavors of these relatively bland meats are very susceptible to being veiled by a sauce, far more so than beef, lamb, game, and other strong-flavored meats.

Lobster is a good example. If we plainly boil or broil it and serve it with a modicum of clarified butter, we could pragmatically select a fine wine like a *Grand Cru* Chablis. If, on the other hand, we prepare our lobster the hot and spicy Fra Diavolo-style, I wouldn't recommend anything better than an inexpensive, everyday white wine with robust qualities. Agreed, this modest wine is not in keeping with the finesse of the lobster meat, but that protest is academic because the Fra Diavolo sauce annihilates the lobster's natural delicacy.

Another variable is the character of the ingredients that go into the sauce. Some ingredients, if consumed in sufficient quantities, are clearly hostile to wine (see the subsection titled "Enemies of Wine"). These include the strongly scented herbs, garlic, onions, and other flavoring agents that are abundantly used in Mediterranean-type sauces. Acidy substances like tomatoes and lemon juice also make those Mediterranean-type sauces interfere with the enjoyment of a fine wine.

Still another variable to consider is the quantity of the sauce we consume. A tenth of a dab of assertive horseradish sauce will probably do only slight harm to our appreciation of a fine wine, but we can expect the opposite when we smother our entrée in unseasoned butter sauce, an otherwise decent fellow.

For the most part, a white sauce suggests a white wine and a brown sauce a red wine, but our task is much more complicated than that convenient rule may suggest.

The richer the sauce, whether white or brown, the fuller bodied the wine should probably be. Thus, think of serving a full-bodied white wine with a creamy white sauce and a not so full white with a velouté sauce. Don't forget also to consider such other factors as the cooking ingredients, the method of cooking, the sauce medium, and of course the seasonings. Generally, the stronger the sauce is flavored, the more essential it is that the wine possess most or all of these characteristics: body, firmness, assertiveness, robustness, fruitiness, and acidity.

Another rule of thumb is: The more refined and/or complex a sauce, the more refined and/or complex the wine— but, again, keep in mind the other factors.

Vinaigrette sauce may or may not be harmful to wine. The variables are discussed in the subsection titled "Serving a Salad," on page 23.

The potential sauce problem doesn't end when the dish leaves the kitchen. Mark well those flavoring agents some diners pour on at the table, much to the displeasure of some cooks, which include salt, pepper, and such bottled condiments as mustard, ketchup, and Worcestershire sauce.

Cooking with Wine

The focus of this book is serving wine with food rather than cooking food with wine, which is another subject, demanding its own full-scale volume. However, since aspects of wine cookery interrelate with wine-food affinities, some limited discussion seems appropriate and necessary.

Cookbooks teem with recipes calling for wine. Most of us are very familiar with many of these preparations, including such famous dishes as Beef à la Bourguignonne, Coq au Vin, and Moules à la Marinière. Many a soup recipe also calls for a last-second lacing of sherry or Madeira. Numerous sauces—of which the well-known Bordelaise is one—also make effective use of wine.

Traditionalists assert that the wine in the dish and the one in the wineglass must be identical. We must, they say, drink a Chambertin with Coq au Vin Chambertin and a Riesling with a Coq au Vin Riesling. I don't think that precise match-ups are all that important so long as we have a near match-up. With Coq au Vin Chambertin, for instance, I believe that most of the other Côte de Nuits Burgundies (as well as some other reds) would be adequate. If only a smidgen of wine is used in the recipe, you can take even more liberty in choosing a different drinking wine than the one you used in the dish.

What is of utmost importance is the quality of the wine we use. By quality, I don't necessarily mean we need superb quality (in fact, I think that is a waste of good money). I am only arguing that we should avoid cooking with a wine of inferior quality. To use a poor wine is undesirable because most of the liquid components of a wine (including the alcohol) evaporate when cooked, leaving behind a concentration of the wine's underlying flavor. If that wine was good, you'll have a good residue. If that wine was bad, you'll have a bad residue. It's as simple as that.

The second conclusive reason you shouldn't use an inferior wine is that it doesn't make sense in terms of the investment you've made in the dish's other ingredients, not to mention the value of your time spent in preparing the dish.

Among your worst options is using one of those so-called cooking wines found on supermarket shelves. They came into popularity in the 1920s during Prohibition when real wine wasn't available (at least to conscientious law-abiding citizens). Certain people got so used to their terrible flavor that these "wines" remain in vogue even today, nearly half a century after repeal.

Another common error made in the typical American kitchen concerns the quantity of wine used. A lot of amateur cooks think that since a little wine is good, a lot would be even better. Never. A wine should enhance, not overpower, the other cooking ingredients.

The time to add the wine depends on your purpose. With a preparation like Sauerbraten, the wine-enriched marinade is added to the meat days before the dish is cooked (but a marinade, as I discussed before, precludes the serving of a fine wine). With stews, the wine should be added right after the meat is seared—or, at the very least, no less than thirty minutes before the end of the cooking process. When basting with wine, use it at appropriate intermittent moments during the roasting process. With soups, the fortified wine is added at the last second, but only in minute quantities (oh, how many cooks, in homes and restaurants alike, oversherry their soups!).

Leftover wine that has become just a little bit too acidic for drinking pleasure is surprisingly suitable for cooking. While the developed acid makes the wine less than ideal for drinking, the acid serves the same general flavoring purpose as lemon juice and vinegar, two ingredients that one frequently finds in recipes. Because of its acid content, leftover wine is also excellent for marinades—but again, only so long as the wine hasn't become too sourish. A more complete discussion of the subject of leftover wines can be found in Part II on page 79.

Serving More Than One Wine

With most meals, you and I are usually content to serve a single wine, usually with the main course. There are times, however, when it is nice to enjoy two or more wines, provided we don't mind the added chore of washing extra glasses. Our more-than-one-wine dinner is especially appropriate when we have enough people to allow the opening of more than one bottle—and if we are going to uncork them, why not have a variety rather than several bottles of the identical wine? One wine could be served with the hors d'oeuvres, another with the main course, and possibly a third with dessert. Or we could dispense with the hors d'oeuvres and dessert wines and simply serve two wines with the main course. These two wines could be from two different regions or perhaps from the same vineyard but of a different year. But don't make head-on comparisons that would be unfair to one or both of the wines, as would be the case if you pitted a fine Médoc against an equally grand Côte de Nuits. The Bordeaux wine would probably be overwhelmed by the bigness of the Côte de Nuits, which in turn would seem a little too unsophisticated and straightforward when compared with the Bordeaux. Your best course of action in these cross-tastings is to select wines with enough similarities that their truly unique qualities become readily apparent.

Still another possibility is to have a full-scale formal dinner with many courses with wines to match. This subject is discussed separately on pages 29–34.

The order in which you serve two or more wines can be reasonably determined by following these time-honored guidelines:

White before red
Dry before sweet
Light before full
Youth before age
Least before best

Serving a white before a red wine is generally sound advice because in almost every instance the red's complex and assertive character would impare your palate's ability fully to appreciate whatever subtleties the white has to offer.

Drinking the dry before the sweet wine is also a good idea. Sweet flavors are counterproductive early in the meal because they stun our palate's capacity for detecting subtle nuances and they dull rather than excite our appetite. That is why desserts are traditionally served at the meal's conclusion. The next time you have an opportunity to cross-taste a bone-dry and medium-dry white wine, conduct this test: Sip the bone-dry wine, then the medium-dry one, then go back to the bone-dry wine. You'll discover that most of the delicate statement of the drier wine will vanish. When determining the degree of dryness or sweetness of a wine, don't take the label's definition at face value. The popular Dry Sack sherry, for instance, is too sweet to be objectively classified as dry.

Pitting a full-bodied wine against a light-bodied wine is like matching a heavyweight against a lightweight boxer. In all likelihood, the heavyweight will overpower the smaller opponent, not giving the lighter fighter an opportunity to display his boxing finesse. If you want to be able to appreciate what the lighter bodied of two wines has to offer, you must serve and savor it before sampling the fuller wine.

The youth-before-age rule is suggested because a wine at its prime will usually make any underdeveloped qualities in a younger, less mature wine quite obvious. By old, I mean mature, not senile. As with the youthful wine, the over-the-hill wine should be served before the wine that is at its peak—otherwise, the old wine's negative qualities will be magnified. Don't think of youth versus age in terms of absolute years. Most Beaujolais are old after a few years while a Château Latour of a great vintage can still be immature after fifteen years.

The final of our five sequence rules—least before best—doesn't need very much explanation, though I've run across more than a few wine drinkers in my life who served the best wine first while saving the worst till the last. They reasoned that their guests would be so pickled by the conclusion of the meal that they wouldn't know the difference between a lousy and a fine wine. If one drinks in moderation, the higher quality wine tastes better when served later because its superior qualities will become more apparent after drinking the lesser wine. Conversely, the lesser wine will usually be enjoyed more before our palates have a chance to sample the better wine.

Of course you will find that these five rules sometimes conflict, but don't be dismayed, because all it takes is a little common sense to set the right priorities. Let us examine the case of a French Sauternes. Although it is white, the "dry before sweet" rule logically supersedes the "white before red" rule because of the wine's explosive sweetness.

What You Drink or Eat Beforehand

Your perception of the flavor and smell of a wine can be significantly altered by what you have previously eaten or drunk. To prove this phenomenon for yourself, make this test with any slightly sweet wine: Observe how the wine tastes sweeter after you've licked a lemon—and how the wine loses its sweetness and may even become sourish after you've sucked a sugar cube. While you probably won't be encountering such extreme taste distortions in your normal wining and dining experiences, some degree of distortion will always be perceptible, at least to an educated palate.

The Type of Course

When selecting a wine for a particular course, you must take into consideration what was consumed beforehand, as I mentioned in the preceding section. And if your dinner is to be harmoniously orchestrated in its entirety, your selection of foods and wines for a particular course must anticipate and enhance the foods and wines that are to follow in later courses. Needless to say, this is not an easily mastered technique, but acquiring a basic understanding is not all that difficult.

Let us start with the first course—or at least what sometimes precedes the first course: the half-century-old American-invented tradition of serving cocktails before dinner. This custom is an abomination to any great wine—but if you are merely having a good wine, one standard-sized cocktail won't doom your taste buds. To be sure, you will lose some taste perception, but the trade-off of enjoying your predinner cocktail, should you enjoy one, will probably more than compensate for the slight sensory impairment. If you decide you want to reduce that damage, you might bear in mind that certain cocktails are worse than others as far as the palate is concerned. Those to stay away from are the sweet and/or sour mixed-drink concoctions, such as the Manhattan; those containing bitters or other piquant flavorings, such as the Bloody Mary; those incorporating soda or tonic (it's best to drink your booze neat or with water); and those laden with highly acidic juices, such as the Screwdriver and, again, our friend the Bloody Mary. Ironically, the much-maligned Martini is one of the best predinner drinks as far as wine drinking is concerned. And between the gin Martini and the vodka Martini, the latter is preferable because of the absence of the juniper-berry flavoring. Scotch and the lighter single-malt whiskeys are also suitable, but their relatively forceful flavor sometimes gets in the way of the subsequent enjoyment of a wine.

If you really want to protect your palate, I would suggest forgoing cocktails altogether and sipping—as is the growing custom in America—these wines:

- Dry white (French Chablis, etc.)
- Brut or natural Champagne (if nonassertive)
- Dry vermouth (especially if produced in Chambéry, France)
- Kir (dry white wine with a touch of cassis)
- Dry sherry (Fino, Amontillado, etc.)
- Dry Madeira (Sercial or possibly the not as dry Rainwater)

When selecting a Champagne, remember that "dry," or "sec," is, in reality, a little sweet. Purchase "brut" if you wish dry, and "natural" if you wish bone-dry Champagne.

A number of other beverages—such as a dry Montilla, or white Port—are equally suitable, though their popularity in the United States is not quite as high as those in the list that I just presented. The watchwords are dry and nonassertive.

Beer, of course, should never be drunk as a predinner beverage unless you plan to imbibe with your meal a rather ordinary wine, the type that has few qualities worth protecting.

If you should happen to drink a sweet or very assertive predinner beverage, your best course of action is to eliminate all alcoholic beverages during your appetizer and soup courses, thereby giving your palate a chance to regain some of its sensitivity.

Out of consideration for the food and wines that are to follow, you must select your hors d'oeuvres, if they are served, judiciously. There are many culinary ogres, but the ones that seem to occur most often are fishy appetizers, such as anchovy-topped tidbits; vinegary foods, such as pickles; oily concoctions, such as dips; and piquant goodies, including deviled eggs and Guacamole. Those artificially flavored snack crackers and chips are equally as malevolent to your enjoyment of a subsequent wine.

If you are the host or hostess, responsible for selecting the foods, when you sit down at the table for the appetizer course, chances are you can continue to serve the same wine that you served with the predinner hors d'oeuvres. When selecting the appetizer, stay away from wine's natural enemies, such as fruit cocktails, lemony seafood cocktails, and spicy dishes in general. Better choices include items such as pâté, clams or oysters on the half shell, quiche, or simply prepared shrimp. Of course, you don't have to serve a wine with this course—simply serve a predinner drink and a wine with the main course, thereby using the appetizer course as a sort of buffer between the two alcoholic offerings.

After the appetizer comes the main course or, in some instances, one or more of these courses: soup, pasta, fish.

If you serve soup, I really don't think a wine is all that necessary. A glass of wine and a bowl of soup are somewhat incompatible because the combination of the two liquids does not contribute sufficient contrast in texture. A wine is in order if the soup is thick and hearty or if the soup has been laced with fortified wine, such as a dry sherry or Madeira (in this case, serve the wine that went into the soup). If you do decide to serve a wine and don't want the expense and bother of opening another bottle, you may consider carrying over the appetizer wine (if you served one) into the soup course. Or you may serve the wine you plan to serve with the next course. Needless to say, with both these methods, your carry-over wine must be compatible with both the soup and the preceding or following course.

Eating pasta before the main entrée is a popular custom in Italy (in America we tend to treat pasta as the main entrée or as a starch accompaniment to the main entrée). Since pasta per se is basically neutral, it is the sauce that is the primary determinant for the wine for this course.

Preceding the main entrée with a fish course is also

popular in Europe, especially in France and Italy. Generally, the fish course requires a fullish white in order to stand up to the wine(s) served with the previously consumed hors d'oeuvres. Another reason for the preference of a fullish white is that a lighter bodied white would probably present too much of a contrast with the upcoming red wine that you will probably be serving with the meat dish, your next course.

In today's American cornucopia-shopping world, you have an incredible choice of main entrées that you can prepare. As discussed in an earlier section of this book, your choice of wine will be largely determined by a combination of factors that include the primary ingredient, the cooking method, and the sauce.

If you want, you can simultaneously serve two red (or two white) wines with your main course—but serve the star wine only after your guests have had at least a five- or ten-minute opportunity to savor the first red by itself. Otherwise, the first red may seem too inconsequential, not because of its quality per se, but because of its quality relative to the finer wine.

Your selection and preparation of the vegetables that will accompany your main course must be done knowledgeably, especially if you are serving a fine wine. If you are, season your vegetables with a light hand and generally avoid strongly flavored produce such as cabbage, turnips, brussels sprouts, spinach, and beets. More preferable are lightly buttered peas and—for the starch accompaniment—parsleyed boiled potatoes. You have many alternatives, including snow peas, carrots, cauliflower, string beans—if fresh, young, and delicately seasoned. As a starch alternative to potatoes, you may serve plainly cooked rice or that delicious French bean favorite, flageolet. An oven-warmed crusty French bread can be served on the side, but outside of a nibble or two, save all or most of it for the cheese, should you serve that dairy product at or near the conclusion of your meal.

The issue of when and if salad greens are to be served is explored in the next section.

The next course of the typical American meal is a sweet dessert, but the serving of cheese and/or fruit in place of sugary concoctions is growing in popularity. The encyclopedia section of this book gives you appropriate suggestions for a number of different desserts, cheeses, or fruits. Bear in mind that in a normal day-to-day meal you don't necessarily have to serve a wine for this course, but it can add a little charm on special occasions. In the case of cheese, serving wine is almost a must because wine and cheese often bring out the best in each other. When serving cheese (alone or accompanied by a bowl of suitable fruits), consider carrying over the bottle of wine you served with the main course, especially if that bottle was a red wine, the fuller bodied, the better.

You'll find other tips and insights concerning the meat course in the section on formal dinirg (pages 29–34) as well as in their appropriate places elsewhere in this book.

Serving a Salad

One of the most contested battlegrounds of wine-food affinities among epicures is salad. Do you serve the salad greens at a meal, and if so, when and with what type of dressing?

I personally don't believe that salad greens coated with an acid-based dressing have any place in a dinner that features a great wine, unless that salad is consumed at the meal's conclusion, after the diner has finished his or her wine drinking.

My belief does not imply, however, that you shouldn't

serve a salad at a meal that is accompanied by a wine of less than fine pedigree. On the contrary, salads do add character to a meal and, in the case of a hearty repast, balance and refreshment. For most of the meals we eat, a salad should pose no problem to our wine if we follow six basic guidelines.

First, avoid well-seasoned salad dressings, such as Russian and blue cheese, and stick with a simple, intelligently made vinaigrette. When preparing the latter salad dressing, never make the oil-to-vinegar ratio less than 4:1, as I find in most American homes and restaurants. If you can make the ratio 6:1 or even a wee bit higher, all the better (if you're using the freshest and best of oils—such as a high-grade walnut or olive oil—this ratio is pleasing). Second, avoid malt or cider vinegar and use wine vinegar instead. Even better, substitute lemon or lime juice for the vinegar. You can also replace the vinegar with dry white wine, but this makes the salad dressing too bland for my taste. Third, if you dry your salad greens sufficiently before adding the dressing, less dressing will be needed to coat the leaves, and, in the process, your acid intake is reduced. Fourth, get into the habit of cleaning your palate with a piece of bread or bites of food such as potato or meat in between nibbles of the salad and sips of the wine. Fifth, consider serving the salad before the wine (again, you'll have to cleanse your palate with an appropriate food) or as a separate course after the wine is finished, as is the custom in some parts of Europe. Finally, remember that a fullish, robust, everyday wine will fare best against a vinaigrette-tainted palate.

Your Guests and the Occasion

Quite frequently, a dinner may take on added proportions, becoming a special event because of a guest and/or the occasion. Either of these two situations may then become a more important wine-selection determinant than the food.

If the dinner is meant to impress a client, boss, or lover, perhaps you may talk yourself into serving a better bottle of wine than your budget or quality of food calls for. Or you may opt for a safe wine choice, one that has proven to be agreeable to you on previous encounters or one that you can discuss with savoir faire, having studied the vineyard's exciting history. In those cases, I say go ahead if it pleases you, because your goal for the night is probably seduction or making a sale rather than happily marrying the wine with the food.

More often, however, your nonfood motivation for selecting a wine is to please rather than impress your guests. You may serve a particular wine because it is your guest's favorite or of the same year of his or her birth, marriage, or divorce. Perhaps the wine is the one your guest has always wanted to sample—or the one you sampled with him or her seven summers ago on a memorable evening in Paris. Or maybe the person is such a good friend that you decided to open the finest bottle in your cellar.

Your guest's wine knowledge and level of appreciation is also a criterion. Unless he or she is a very good friend (and sometimes even then), it's generally considered a culinary crime to open up a fine bottle for a wine neophyte. It is ironic that with some less than knowledgeable guests you are often more likely to impress them with a cheap imported French wine (so long as it has a fancy label) than with a costly wine from a top-quality California vineyard, such as a David Bruce or Mayacamas. Even if such guests are types who are not easily impressed by fancy-looking labels, their palates would probably better enjoy a simple, easy-to-understand wine than a complex great wine because the appreciation of the latter is an acquired, cultivated taste. (Any inexperienced wine drinker who tells you that he honestly prefers a fine Château Lafite-Rothschild over a fine Beaujolais has probably only convinced himself that the first tastes better, since he knows it is supposed to taste better.) On the other hand, if your guest can appreciate and intelligently discuss the virtues of a fine wine, then the pleasures you derive from any expensive wine you open will be greatly enhanced.

Another component in your decision process is the mood you anticipate your guest will be in. A fine wine is wasted in the midst of gloom, despair, depression, hostility, boredom, and other negative mental states. A genteel environment, on the other hand, improves any decent wine.

Try to predict the personal taste preferences of your guest as well. Some people simply like sweetish wines, and the opening of a fine white Corton would only displease them.

The worst type of dinner guest is the wine snob, that bore who has memorized a lot of facts about wine without fully understanding them. (This is quite easy and is often done in the sport of wine-imbibing one-upmanship.) Not only does the snob blindly follow the wine-food affinity rules like a juggernaut, he can become a little precious. He or she will tell you, for instance, that a more rugged wine is called for to drink with the left rather than the right leg of a wild turkey because the bird perches on his left leg, causing a circulation problem that in turn toughens the meat. Or he might try to convince you that while a 1961 Cos d'Estournel is perfect for a male pheasant, you simply must open a 1966 Cos d'Estournel for a female pheasant. Your best defense against this bore is not to invite him into your home in the first place. If the mistake has already been committed, then lock him in a closet and let him entertain his favorite person, himself.

Of less harm to your meal than the wine snob is the guest who scoffs at your dedicated efforts to find a suitable wine-food match-up. He or she claims it makes no difference. Before contemptuously trying to put this so-called iconoclast in his place, we must remember that his views—and not ours—are in the majority. Well over half the wine-drinking people in this world are peasants and other common folk who couldn't give a damn about what wine goes best with what food—and, in my opinion, the majority of them enjoy their wine drinking more than most of us who can afford the sometimes added time and cost of matching wines with food. If we told them about our devotion to finding the best wine, they would chuckle just as much as we would if we heard that someone was trying to find out which cola drink went best with a Big Mac.

Next time you invite the "it doesn't matter" guest to dinner, indulge him or her by pandering to his deeply rooted belief. Serve the person (but not yourself) the sweetish Liebfraumilch—after all, an advertisement of one of the importers claims it goes well with everything. For this type of wine drinker, it probably does.

If one of your guests has an eccentricity such as loving to plunk an ice cube in his wine, let him. Tens of millions of other nonfussy wine drinkers throughout the world (including France and Italy) commit this and other gourmet improprieties, such as diluting wine with water, so why should we be so uppity? We shouldn't take situations like these with alarm because wine drinking should never be taken too seriously. Just don't waste your good wine on him or her.

Not to be confused with a wine snob is the person who genuinely enjoys the subject of wine and who relishes discussing it with (and, if he is considerate, only with) others who share his deep interest. Such conversation is just as stimulating as when two other devotees of any other field get together, whether these people be Egyptologists comparing notes on Middle Kingdom architecture or baseball fans talking about Hank Aaron's home-run record.

In addition to considering your guest, judge the occasion. If it is a holiday dinner, such as on Thanksgiving or Christmas, you have a good reason to spend a few more dollars on a bottle of wine than the food calls for. On such festive family get-togethers, sometimes Champagne is the perfect choice because of its traditional association with gaiety.

Generally speaking, the more elaborate the meal, the better your wine should be. Conversely, the more ordinary the repast, the more ordinary the wine should be. This attitude makes culinary sense because a great wine will not add that much to an ordinary meal, and, in the process, the ordinary meal will do little to benefit the fine wine. Even if an everyday meal didn't distort the delicate qualities of a Château Lafite-Rothschild, that combination would be just as inappropriate as it would be for a billionaire to be gardening in a four-hundred-dollar suit. He could certainly afford the extravagance, but what would be the advantage? His escapade would also diminish his Dapper Dan pleasure whenever he dressed up for a special occasion.

For gala dinners more effort is justified in matching the wine with the food, but not to the degree to which this is carried by some European gourmet societies. A small committee meets a few days before the banquet to test various wines against each dish. To me this is overkill because the food served at those banquets is seldom cooked anywhere near perfection, despite what certain ill-informed reporters may tell you. With so many mouths to feed, the kitchen is, out of sheer necessity, a factorylike assembly-line operation that must take numerous preparation shortcuts as well as cook certain dishes ahead of their proper time.

The Weather

Weather should also play a role in your wine selection. I vividly remember a particularly hot midday in Tahiti when I was having a light, summery meal on the deck of a harbor-anchored yacht. My captain and host—God bless him—served a 1955 Château Lafite-Rothschild. His choice had pizzazz, and it flattered me, but it lacked appropriateness. Given the weather conditions, a chilled, refreshingly light wine of good but unpretentious qualities such as a better than average, light-bodied red of Provence or Beaujolais-Villages would have been more satisfying, and therefore more suitable.

The Full-Fledged Formal Dinner

While most of us in today's fast-paced world seldom if ever sit down to an elaborate, six- or eight-course formal dinner, it can be a pleasant occasion that we should consider experiencing at least once during our earthly stay, if for no other reason than for enjoying this elegant moment of life.

A key to these dinners is not to take them too seriously. I have known too many people who, influenced by Hollywood movies, have injected into the dinner elements of stuffiness and strained formality, two qualities that should have been locked up in the Victorian attic where they belong. Instead, I strongly suggest that you invite only your warmest friends and enjoy them and the meal, formality for formality's sake be damned.

Another element of success is simplicity. Instead of thinking in terms of preparing fancy dishes that will visually awe your guests, concentrate on buying the best and freshest ingredients, cooking them properly, and—for the sake of flavor, aroma, and texture—serving the dishes without delay. Let the natural flavors of the raw ingredients speak for themselves.

The dishes selected should be on the delicate side, especially during the early and middle stages of the dinner in order to prevent your palate from becoming needlessly tired.

If you crave a robust dish, satisfy that desire during a standard three-course meal.

Naturally, when orchestrating our formal dinner, we must call to mind the various guidelines discussed in the preceding sections and throughout this book, including those regarding sequence. This section will elaborate on those considerations that especially pertain to formal dinners.

Every quarter of the gourmet world has its own fixed version on the progressive steps of a formal dinner. Rather than overtax you with all the possible ramifications, allow me to give you one that is both widely accepted and practical:

Predinner drinks
Appetizer
Soup
Fish
Meat
Cheese
Dessert
Coffee
Brandy

Strongly flavored and/or high-alcohol-content predinner drinks have no place before a formal dinner—and that means not even one. It would be a waste of time and money to produce such a dinner for even slightly debilitated palates. Unless one is firmly addicted to his predinner Martini or Scotch drink, it shouldn't be that difficult to abstain from these palate impairers for the rare, special occasion of a full-fledged formal dinner. Besides, in our formal dinner, we'll have sufficient quantities of alcohol as it is. The classic choice of predinner drinks (if you elect to have one) for a formal meal is a nonassertive brut Champagne, though the other predinner wines listed on page 20 would also be suitable if knowledgeably selected.

Because of the length of the meal, the hors d'oeuvres (if any) should be light and nonfilling. Food with more than a trace of vinegar or citrus as well as any of the other enemies of wine should be avoided.

As mentioned earlier, the soup course doesn't have to have an accompanying wine, though many people (not I) insist on it for the occasion of a formal dinner.

Some hosts feel that having both a soup and a fish course is incompatible with today's life-style. If you agree, then feel free to eliminate one of these courses from your formal dinner, though you will be subtracting a little—but not much—of the magic of your special dinner.

The sherbet (*sorbet,* in France) serves a specific function: It helps cleanse the palate between courses. My quarrel with this procedure is that the sherbet's sweetness may disrupt your palate for the courses yet to come. Though you can insert this course at several places, some epicures believe that it seems most suitable between the fish and the meat courses. Some fifteen-course meals have inserted the sherbet course two or more times, but I don't think this will concern most of us.

Your meat course can be red meat or poultry, depending on your preference. I personally maintain that a stronger flavored meat such as beef, lamb, or game is superior because this provides a better change of pace from the previous fish course.

The order and interrelationship of the next two courses—cheese and dessert—are hotly debated issues, with the battle line more or less drawn in the middle of the English Channel. Most French gourmets are accustomed to serving the cheese immediately after the meat course for a very practical reason. The fine red wine served with the meat course can be carried over into the cheese course, thus allowing for a felicitous match. This sequence makes culinary sense too.

The English, on the other hand, prefer to serve the cheese after the dessert and to eat the cheese with, ideally, a vintage Porto wine—particularly if the cheese to be served is a mature Stilton or a quality, well-aged Cheddar-type. I personally like the French method, though my insatiable love for variety makes the English approach enjoyable from time to time.

Another popular approach I enjoy is serving the cheese with a bowl of compatible fruit. Without fruit, a red wine is more often than not your best bet with a cheese offering

The dessert course can be of two basic types. Fruit (so long as you haven't served it with the cheese course) or a concocted sweet dish such as a Peach Melba. Again, for the sake of variety, I enjoy both alternatives, but I find myself choosing fresh fruits in the vast majority of instances. My reason is that concocted sweet dishes tend to be a little too rich and heavy after a sizable meal, whereas fruits if properly selected have the capacity to cut the heaviness of the preceding course, thereby adding rather than interfering with the meal as a whole. (For fruit suggestions, see the entry "Fruit" in the encyclopedia section.) Sweet desserts, I believe, are better suited to normal meals—or even better, as a midafternoon or late evening treat with friends, as is the custom in the Middle East and many other parts of the world.

If you elect to serve a concocted sweet dessert, some gourmets insist upon a dish with more flair than, say, a slice of pie or a dish of ice cream. I guess showmanship is okay for this course of our formal dinner, so why not? Some of the popular choices are:

- Baked Alaska
- Bavarian Cream
- Cherries Jubilee
- Crème Brûlée
- Crêpes Suzette

- Croquembouche (if no chocolate)
- Floating Island or Oeufs à la Neige
- Fruit tarts
- Mont-Blanc
- Peach Melba
- Zabaglione
- Zuppa Inglese

Of these choices, the custard-type dishes (Crême Brûlèe and Oeufs a la Neige) and the fruit tarts work best. For reasons previously explained, stay away from chocolate-based dishes—Chocolate Mousse, Sachertorte, and the like. The same is true for banana-, pineapple-, and citrus-based dishes.

As for the choice of wine for the dessert course, quality French Sauternes is my favorite choice—especially with fruits. I am also partial to a sweet, quality Champagne, a Hungarian Tokay of at least five *puttonyos*, or a German wine of Beerenauslese credentials (a Trockenbeerenauslese should be savored alone). With the concocted sweet dishes, the sweet Sauternes-type wines and sweet Champagnes are okay, but the ingredients of the dish must be taken into consideration. If, for instance, you're serving Zabaglione, drink a sweet Marsala wine. If the dessert is especially rich in sugar or if it is dominated by a particular flavoring, consider serving a suitable liqueur in place of wine. Kirschwasser, to cite an example, would probably go well with a cherry torte.

Immediately following the dessert and cheese course, some people serve a fine Porto wine, perhaps with a few nuts, such as walnuts. Though this custom is nice and prolongs the meal, I don't believe that its absence would be that noticeable from an overall point of view.

Next comes the coffee. The brew should be freshly made, strong (espresso, *café filtre*, etc.) and served in demitasses. Offering your guest coffee in the normal-sized coffee cup is literally gross for a fine dining occasion. No wine should ever be served with coffee, a natural enemy. Some people combine the coffee and liqueur phase of the dinner, but I'm against that custom because both of these liquid refreshments can be best enjoyed by themselves.

Following coffee, a snifter of your favorite Cognac is savored—perhaps after you have adjourned from the dining room into the living room. Classic accompaniments to the Cognac are profound afterdinner discussions and fine cigars. (You should discreetly inquire about the possible objections from smoke-hating guests, but try to enlighten them that it is an inferior cigar that is chiefly responsible for giving cigar smoke its bad reputation.)

Don't think that Cognac is the only suitable afterdinner drink. For a pleasing change of pace, try a top-quality Armagnac or Calvados, for instance. Even a vintage Porto or Madeira makes a fine choice now and then. But I wouldn't suggest a liqueur. While one might be okay after a normal meal, it would be too sweet after the full-scale formal dinner. A Cognac (or Cognac-type drink), on the other hand, puts a refreshing finish to your multihour repast. And the better the Cognac, the better the finish.

You probably noticed that I haven't discussed when to serve the salad. In a formal dinner, out of consideration for the fine wines, a salad should not be served. Besides, with so many other courses being offered, a salad would be out of place and outflanked. Save your salads for less than formal dinners.

Serving a Great Wine

Most of the time we try to match the wine with the dish. Whenever we plan to have a great wine, the process should be reversed. We try to match the food with the great wine because the latter's nuances are so easily eclipsed.

Since there are so few great wines in this world, to drink one under less than ideal circumstances is a mortal sin, at least to my mind. Ideal circumstances mean not only serving the proper food but having the right quests (knowledgeable and articulate), mood (relaxed and unhurried), lighting (subdued candlelight), and glasses (large and perfect specimens).

In order to have the great wine show off its finest qualities, it is also very important to serve the right wine that will precede and/or accompany the great wine. This foil should be high in quality and reasonably similar in character to the great wine. If our great wine is a 1955 Château Lafite-Rothschild, we might choose a wine like a 1966 Château Beychevelle.

Design a simple accompanying meal devoid of strong flavors. Sometimes a great red wine is most at home with a suitable cheese, period.

What would I serve you if you gave me a great wine? If you gave me a great Médoc, such as a 1955 Château Latour, perhaps I would prepare a roast rack of baby lamb or a milk-fed veal roast. With a great Côte de Nuits Burgundy, I may offer you a simply prepared rare-roasted beef tenderloin or a young venison sirloin roast, again cooked on the rarish side. With a fine dry white like a Montrachet, my offering would be a poached striped bass in a delicate wine sauce. Your costly gift of Trockenbeerenauslese would be served, as I mentioned before, without food—but your Château d'Yquem would be served with ripe stone-pit fruits, such as peaches and nectarines at the peak of their season. Your Château Cheval Blanc or Château Ausone, from Saint-Emilion, or a Château Petrus, of Pomerol, would be lovely with a roasted pheasant. Your fine old Italian Barolo would come off well with wild boar, while your fifteen-year-old Chianti Classico would display its charm best with a soft-ripened cheese like a Taleggio.

What would you serve me if I gave you these wines? I hope

your choices would be a little different from mine, for that makes wine drinking and discussion more interesting.

Differences Between Two Seemingly Identical Wines

When following a suggestion for a specific wine to go with a specific dish, bear in mind that wines of the same or similar names can differ, sometimes markedly. The most famous example is Vouvray, from France's Loire Valley. Depending on the year, that wine can be sparkling or still, dry or sweet, acidy or flabby, thin- or full-bodied, short- or long-lived, good or bad.

Even an identical grape variety yields different wines in different climates, soils, and topography. To illustrate, let's compare the French Chablis with Pouilly-Fuissé. While both are made exclusively from the Chardonnay grape, Chablis is tarter than Pouilly-Fuissé, primarily because the Chablis vineyards are located, as the bird flies, some one hndred miles farther north, thereby having less of the sun that develops the natural sugar in the grape. Sometimes two adjoining vineyards produce entirely different wines because the soil and topography vary tremendously in a matter of just a few meters. Château Bellevue is contiguous to the celebrated Château d'Yquem in Bordeaux's Sauternes district, but Bellevue produces commonplace wine, while the other, ambrosia fit for the gods.

The grape grower and wine producer also influence how the wine will eventually turn out. Some growers and producers are craftsmen who approach their profession with pride and as a labor of love. On the other extreme you find the mass-market-oriented wine people who sacrifice quality for quantity. Louis Latour and Mr. X may both offer Pouilly-Fuissé wine, but Louis Latour's will be superior because his firm puts more money, care, and expertise into the wines that carry his label.

One wine producer's use of the word dry on the label may be the equivalent of another wine firm's medium dry. Labeling a wine drier than is actually the case is a common ploy among mass-market wine producers. They know the typical American wine drinker "talks dry, drinks sweet," meaning that he wants to think he is drinking dry because it is "in," but—having been weaned on Coke—he prefers a sweeter taste.

Some wine firms even make two wines: one for local consumption and one for export. Usually the export version is sweeter, mainly because the overseas market has a sweeter tooth and because the higher sugar content helps mask some of the congenital or transportation-caused imperfections in the wine.

Two bottles of the exact wine may differ because of what has happened when the bottle left the wine producer's cellar or warehouse. You might find a wine ideal for a particular dish, but the bottle you purchase next month may not be quite so perfect because the wine was harmed when being shipped across the Atlantic Ocean. Or perhaps the second bottle was improperly stored in your wine merchant's basement or main-floor area—or maybe it was displayed for a couple of weeks in the sun-drenched store window.

What takes place after you bring home two identical bottles also matters. One wine may taste sweeter because you served it at a higher temperature—or it may taste more tannic because you didn't decant it or let it breathe sufficiently— or it may taste off because you have had too many predinner cocktails or have a slight cold. Finally, the difference between the two wines may be entirely a product of our creative imagination or faulty memory.

Differences in Individual Taste Perceptions

How many times have you observed two people sitting at the same table drinking the same wine yet describing the wine somewhat differently? One person may think the wine is drier (or whatever) than his friend. Why? There are a number of possible explanations.

First, no two people have exactly the same taste perceptions because no two people have identical physical papillae and olfactory receptors, just as they don't have identical fingerprints. Each of our four basic types of taste buds—salt, sour, sweet, and bitter—and our myriad types of scent receptors react differently in combinations with each other. The difference in our metabolism also changes with age—the older we get, the less acute our taste and odor perceptions. In addition, the threshold of the sensory reactions increases as the temperature of wine decreases—coldness numbs the senses. (Try this test: Notice how much sweeter ice cream tastes when it has melted.)

The above-described taste differences are principally a matter of physiology. Most of the differences between individuals, however, are mental in character. They include wine-drinking education and experience: During the early stages of one's wine-drinking life a person generally prefers sweet wines (bone-dry wines are an acquired taste, so it's ridiculous for a neophyte to pretend he likes bone-dry wine just because it is fashionable). What we have consumed beforehand matters, too. A medium-dry wine will taste dry if preceded by a sweet wine or food—or sweetish, if preceded by a dry wine or sourish food.

Another determinant of how we evaluate a wine—especially in terms of quality—is our preconceived notions: If we think a wine will be good or bad, the laws of self-fulfilling prophecy often take hold. After all, if we spend twenty bucks for a bottle of wine, it better taste good, or we'll have to admit to ourselves and our friends that we foolishly wasted good money. The name or vintage of the wine also influences us. A very bad bottle of Château Lafite-Rothschild usually seems better to most people than an agreeable *vin ordinaire*. Interestingly, if we soaked off and then switched the labels of these two wines, the reverse would probably be true. The place where we drink a wine also influences our judgment. A wine served in a fancy restaurant or a peaceful terrace over-looking a beautiful valley will seem to taste better than it would back in a small, city apartment.

Regional Match-ups

Contrary to the pronouncements that I have found in some of the regional wine and food books in my library, there are far more important wine-selection considerations than matching up a dish with the wine from the same region. Today, with access to a variety of wines in quality neighborhood wine shops, we can usually find an equally suitable—and sometimes superior—wine to the ones from the region in question. We may be doing our palate a favor if, for instance, we drink a dry French Muscadet de Sèvre-et-Maine rather than a slightly sweet Italian Lacrima Christi with Spaghetti con Vongole (spaghetti with clam sauce), even though that dish is a Campania regional specialty

Nevertheless, the search for regional match-ups has its merits, providing that we have already satisfied the other, more important wine selection factors. Besides adding a charming mystique to a meal, regional match-ups often make sense, too. In fact, when in doubt or when all other determinants are equal, let me be unequivocal in suggesting that you opt for the regional marriage. Whenever such a match-up makes particular sense, I have noted it in the appropriate entry in Part III, the encyclopedia section.

Another argument supporting the validity of regional wine-food affinities is that the local populace tends to develop recipes and wine styles that are mutually harmonious. Thus, these match-ups—when they exist—are not so much a coincidence or myth or regional chauvinism as a design slowly fashioned over hundreds of years.

Some of the more famous regional match-ups include red Burgundy with Beef à la Bourguignonne, Lambrusco with a robust Tortellini Bolognese, and Alsatian Gewürztraminer with a choucroute. But, as I said, there are times when wines from other regions make equal or better substitutes.

The time when regional match-ups are the most logical is when you are traveling abroad. By all means drink the local *vin ordinaire* wines, because they are fresh and available, two situations that probably won't exist when you get back home. When journeying through Burgundy, for instance, you're better off drinking the local wine out of the barrel than a grand Chambertin because you can always buy the latter wine in America, at approximately the same retail price being charged in France.

The Desire to Experiment

One of the joys of wine drinking is exploring the world's incredible variety of distinct wines. I've always felt a little sorry for the person who is unwilling to experiment with different wines and who, instead, sticks almost exclusively to a limited list of his or her tried and true favorites. You know the type of person I'm talking about—the one who orders the same two or three wines practically every time he or she visits a liquor store or restaurant. Please don't get me wrong—I'm not disagreeing with a person's right to choose what he wants. Nor am I finding fault with his loyalty, an admirable trait. I just think that such a person is missing out on some of the fun of wine drinking.

Perhaps the most pitiful nonexperimenter is the individual who, out of fear of being wrong, puts into execution the "Champagne and rosé goes with everything" rule. While a Champagne and rosé do go with a broad selection of dishes, there are only a few instances in which they are one of your best alternatives. Besides, a rosé wine by its birthright is never distinguished and therefore cannot really add anything extraordinary to the dining experience. The same is true with the majority of sparkling wines consumed in this country; they are literally cheap copies of those fine sparkling wines of the French Champagne district (although some other wine regions produce a few noteworthy examples, such as is the case with northern California and its Korbel and Schramsberg brands). Still another drawback to following the "Champagne or rosé" rule is that the overuse of any wine bores your palate, thereby reducing the pleasures of dining.

Finally, the pursuit of matching wine with food gives us an excellent opportunity to broaden our taste experiences and, in the process, the chance of extending our personal list of favorite wines.

Wine Availability

Even if you have in the forefront of your mind the name and vintage of the perfect wine for your dish, your thought is purely academic unless that wine is available.

Availability is a function of several factors, including what your friendly local wine merchant has in stock. Even if he has the exact bottle you want, you must take into consideration the element of time: To give its best, a bottle of wine should be allowed to rest after its shaky journey from the store to your home. An ordinary wine can get by with only a few hours' rest. A sediment-laden red wine requires at least a week's rest, and if it is a rare, great red like a 1929 Château Margaux, you may be wise to give it a two- or three-month quiet nap prior to pulling its cork. White wines require less rest than reds because they don't have sediment, but still, a superior white such as a Les Perrières Meursault should probably be laid aside for a week or two.

At times the state of health or maturity of the wines in your cellar will determine your wine selection. For instance, you may have the right type of wine for a particular dish, but the wine still needs more aging—so you compromise and make a secondary choice. Or you may know or suspect that a particular wine is starting to go over the hill and therefore you intelligently decide to bend the affinity rules a bit in order to enjoy the wine when it is still within reach of its prime. And, as I stated before, if the overmatured wine is a precious one, you should definitely work backward: Select the dish and meal to match the wine, not the other way around.

The temperature of your available wine is a major consideration. We haven't done ourselves a favor if we are ready to drink a Heitz Pinot Chardonnay with a fish dish without having planned ahead to allow time to chill the wine to its proper serving temperature.

Your Budget

If you are serving a fine dish that calls for a fine wine and are unable to serve such a wine because of budgetary reasons, then don't worry. Serve a dish with a less than perfect though suitable wine and let the dish be the star for the night.

Calories

A few people that I have lunched with have preferred white to red wine because of a mistaken belief that it's better for the waistline. This is an old wives' tale because the average dry red (approximately 96 calories per four-ounce portion) has only a few calories more than the average dry white wine (88 calories), too little of a difference to justify choosing the white for weight-watching reasons.

The more significant variable as far as calories are concerned is the sweetness of the wine, not the color. A sweet white can have over 50 percent more calories than a dry red.

A dry wine—red or white—is innocent enough to a diet-conscious diner when compared to a bottle of beer (150 calories), a glass of milk (160 calories), a can of Coca-Cola (140 calories), or a restaurant-sized Martini (200 to 300 calories, not counting the olive).

From a general health point of view, wine in moderation is beneficial to one's well-being, advises many a physician, including my own. However, I wouldn't get too excited about the nutrients, vitamins, and minerals provided by a glass of wine—it has some, but they are not significant compared with those of most other foods. Where wine gives the human race the most benefit is in its capacity to make us relax during a meal, thereby reducing tension and abetting our digestive processes. The alcoholic content of the wine—usually 10 to 14 percent—also makes us feel good, which is not a bad by-product either.

Wine Tastings

This type of event doesn't call for food except in an ancillary sense. All you really need is freshly baked French bread or plain water wafers to cleanse your palate in between sips.

Though it's frequently done, cheese should never be served when you are conducting a serious wine tasting—and particularly so when the wines are of superior quality. But, if your purpose is to enjoy yourself, why not, as cheese is tasty and will probably satisfy the appetite that the wine creates. My only advice if you do serve cheese for that purpose is to make sure it is a mild one, such as Port Salut or Brie, because the more flavorful cheeses—including the Swiss-types, such as Gruyère, Emmenthaler, or Jarlsberg—can maim your taste buds.

Unless you are a professional taster, keep the number of wines down to five or six. And if you want to learn something from the tastings, select wines that are similar rather than different (cross-tasting a Rhine Riesling with a Chianti will prove little except one's lack of experience in planning wine tastings). For optimum results, select a common theme. For instance, you could have a vertical tasting (the same vineyard but from different vintages) or a horizontal tasting (the same vintage but different vineyards—or the same vineyard and vintage but different negotiants). Another approach is to serve wines from around the world produced from the same grape. Whatever theme you select, try to keep the wines in the same general price range, and, if possible, serve them in the sequence I suggested on page 16.

Give everyone a card so impressions can be recorded. This system not only helps the memory, it increases the enjoyment of the occasion when the participants later compare their opinions.

Whether you choose to hide the labels is up to you, but if you do, don't put any of your guests on the spot unless they enjoy the guessing game and are secure enough not to mind making judgment errors in front of other participants.

Each person should have at least two glasses, as a single

glass doesn't allow head-on comparisons between two wines. Place a pitcher of water on the table so that each participant can rinse out his glass. He can then discard the rinse water into a nearby receptacle, perhaps a bucket or a large pot.

One potential point of confusion to guard against is forgetting which wine is in what glass—this occurs quite frequently. A little tag, color-coded tape, or other temporary marking on the glass can usually solve this problem. Another common pitfall is forgetting to allow sufficient time to chill the wines or to let them breathe.

Because the participant will be sampling only a little from each bottle of wine, you can usually plan on one bottle of a given wine for each ten to fifteen guests. This assumes, of course, that you have five or six wines and that the participants, taken as a whole, will consume only an average quantity of wine.

Dining Alfresco

By its very nature, the act of eating outdoors is usually accompanied by warmer—and sometimes hot—weather, and, as a result, I would not suggest a fine wine. Such a wine would be just as out of place in a casual outdoor setting as would basic black, pearls, and high heels. Besides, your bottle will probably be severely shaken by the time you reach your picnic plot, and your food will likely be well seasoned—both situations being inimical to any decent wine. What you really want is liquid refreshment, a thirst quencher—and in keeping with that purpose, select a low-alcohol-content wine (definitely under 12 percent) because you may be quaffing a lot of it. Also stay clear of sweetish wines because their higher sugar content may cause you physical discomfort by increasing your body temperature.

While your alfresco entertaining does place restrictions on

the range of wines you can select, you still have a fairly wide choice. These include a rosé (here lies one of the crowning moments of this otherwise mundane wine). When selecting a rosé, however, try to buy one of the best ones (Château d'Queria Tavel, etc.). Excellent nonrosé choices include Beaujolais and the red or white Loires, if in the medium-priced range. The medium-rung Alsacian or German Rieslings as well as the better Sylvaners are also fine choices because of their refreshing qualities combined with their relatively low alcohol content. Also very worthy for the occasion are most California jug wines. Stay away from the pop wines and from Sangria—too much sugar. The same is true for a bubbly, sparkling wine, such as Champagne, because of the excessive shaking factor. However, wines with only slight sparkling qualities—like the Vouvrays and the Swiss Neuchâtels of some years—are suitable providing that they are not too sweet.

If you're traveling abroad, definitely match your picnic food with a local wine, and if it was produced just beyond the oak tree, so much the better.

What about glasses? Those readily available, unbreakable, and disposable plastic glasses are the best, but if you only have paper cups, use them—especially if your wine is of everyday quality.

There are times when you enjoy turning your picnic into a gourmet affair, complete with delicately seasoned and pre-pared foods. These occasions do call for a better than ordi-nary wine, but, for the reasons I mentioned above, don't go overboard.

To chill your picnic wine (and it should be chilled even more than normally called for because of the warm outdoor temperature), I have a couple of tricks for you. The easiest one is to place the bottle securely in a running stream or cool pond, if one exists. If not, wrap the bottle in wet newspapers and store it in the shade for a few hours before serving time, as this method works just like an air-conditioner: The evaporating water cools the surrounding air and, in the process, the bottle and the wine inside it.

Wines in a Restaurant

Wining out poses a host of problems, even to sophisticated epicures with decades of experience. If we are to cope successfully with these problems, we must understand them or—at the minimum—be aware of them.

One of the biggest disappointments in ordering wine in a typical American restaurant is the price. Most stateside proprietors inflate their wine prices four to five times greater than the price they paid for it because, each reasons, "If my cocktails are high-profit items with a four- to five-times markup, why not my wines?" If a wine cost a domestic restaurateur two dollars, the bottle would probably cost the customer eight to ten dollars (plus tax and tip). This lamentable pricing policy is generally the exception to the rule in France and Italy, where most owners are satisfied with a much smaller markup, about double the wholesale price. These Europeans look upon wine as a necessary accompaniment to the food they sell, and so they believe the wine should be sold at a reasonable price, if for no other reason than as a courtesy to the customer.

Usually, the best defense against outrageously priced wines is to order the house wine by the glass or carafe—or to order the least expensive wine (the second least expensive wine on a list is usually the one with the biggest markup because many restaurateurs know that the average diner typically knows little about wines and will semiautomatically order this one because he might appear too cheap if he orders the least expensive bottle). Save your enjoyment of better wines for when you can buy them in a retail store; remember that the bottle that cost you ten dollars in a liquor store will probably cost you at least twenty dollars plus several dollars' tip in a restaurant. Or to look at this economic situation from another angle, the money you might spend in the restaurant will buy you two bottles or more of the same wine worth over twenty dollars in a liquor store (what would cost you about fifty dollars in a restaurant). Any way we look at it, wine in an American restaurant is seldom a bargain (I estimate that out of Manhattan's two thousand dining establishments, less than 2 percent have reasonable wine prices).

An effective way to lower the cost of a wine is to pay corkage, if a restaurant allows it. Some restaurants will permit you to bring your own bottle of wine and will furnish setups (the glasses) for a corkage fee of usually three dollars and sometimes five dollars. If the difference between the liquor store and restaurant price for the bottle of wine is merely equal to the corkage fee, you are still ahead of the financial game because you will be basing your 15 to 20 percent tip on just the amount of the corkage fee and not on what the wine bottle would have cost you in the restaurant.

You can figure on even bigger corkage-related savings as the price of the wine increases. Let us take a hypothetical situation where the identical wine retails for $10 in a liquor store and $24 in a restaurant (based on a four-times markup on the $6 wholesale price). If you buy the bottle in the liquor store, your total price in some states would be $14.64 ($10.00 + $3.00 corkage + $1.04 for the 8 percent sales tax on the combined $13.00 purchase + $ .60 for the 20 percent tip on the $3.00 corkage). In contrast, you pay $29.72 in the restaurant ($24.00 + $1.92 for the 8 percent tax + $4.80 for the 20 percent tip). By paying the corkage fee, you save $15.08, enough to purchase an extra bottle of the good wine and still have change in your pocket

Before going on the corkage route, ask the restaurant about its acceptability and fee when making your reservation. Should the wine you wish to bring have sediment, decant it before leaving your home.

Better than paying the corkage is going to the restaurant that allows you to bring your own wine free, either out of courtesy or because the establishment does not have a wine license. These are great restaurants for any true wine lover.

A major problem in selecting a restaurant has to do with the food options. When dining at home, usually everyone is served the same food, making wine selection easier. In a restaurant, different dishes are ordered by different people— or two people may order fish and the other couple filet mignon. The usual solution is to order rosé or Champagne for everyone, but for reasons I've discussed earlier in the book, this is seldom a sensible tactic. A better approach is to order half bottles or half litres of carafe wines, which allows you to select both a red and a white wine. Or you can simply order the four wines by the glass, red and white. If your dining foursome is having an appetizer course, you may consider ordering a full bottle of white wine and a half bottle of red. The four of you would share half of the contents of the bottle of white wine for your appetizers. When the main entrée arrives, those eating fish would continue drinking white wine, and the two beef eaters would be served the half bottle of red. Another alternative is to make a partial compromise by bridging the gap between the two dishes, if they are not chasms apart. For instance, if one person is having a roast chicken and the other roast baby lamb, a light- to medium-bodied red may do the trick. If in another situation one diner is having a lightly seasoned poached chicken breast and the other sole in cream sauce, then a medium- to full-bodied white may be a workable compromise. My decades of wine-drinking experience have proven to me that for every problem we may encounter there is some solution—maybe not the ideal one, but certainly one that is acceptable and that therefore makes the best of a given situation. All it takes is a basic knowledge of wine and its affinities with food, along with a little reasoning power.

Even when we have all the answers on which wines go with what foods, we may find a very limited or poorly selected inventory of wines, as is the case in most American restaurants.

These establishments stock generic Chablis and Burgundy wines, too sweet for some fine dishes. If the wine list is slightly more extensive, it will have the clichés, such as Beaujolais, Pommard, Pouilly-Fuissé—and as clichés, they are usually the worst values (the better French wine-growing regions can produce by law only so much wine, and, therefore, if a wine becomes popular, the laws of supply and demand take hold). Even if these cliché wines were soundly priced (they're not), most wine lists don't tell you very critical facts, such as the vintage, the importer, and the shipper. In most instances, the shipper will not be one of the better ones because a restaurant wants to maximize profits. If the customer doesn't know the difference between two vintages or two shippers selling a Gevrey-Chambertin, for example, the restaurateur will probably opt to sell the less costly of the two for the price the better one could have fetched. Or the restaurateur may be reluctant to stock the better of the two because he would have to charge a slightly higher price than his next-door competitor is charging for the lesser wine—in which case the the customers would equate the price difference with greed rather than with wholesale cost. Either way we lose.

What every restaurant should do, at least to my mind, is to offer a wide range of fairly priced wines. There should be well-chosen, inexpensive red or white carafe wines for those who don't want to spend that much. The diner should also be offered interesting middle-priced wines and, for the well-heeled or celebrating gourmet, fine wines—but again, fairly priced, with a markup of two (or at the very most, three) times the wholesale price.

When you are in an ethnic restaurant, Greek or whatever, it's often a good idea to select the corresponding ethnic wines. Those bottles are often more knowledgeably selected than the Beaujolais, Pouilly-Fuissé, and other standard wine-list items. But if you're dining in a restaurant where you seriously doubt its knowledge of wine selection, whether that spot be ethnic or regional American, you are better off in the long run to order a glass of house wine, or, if you can, bring your own.

Still another problem with ordering wines in restaurants is waiters who are oenological illiterates (most are) but who can get away with their charade because most of their customers are just as ignorant about wine. How many times have I asked a waiter, "What type of wine is your carafe wine?" only to be answered, "It's red." Further probing with questions like, "I know it's red; could you please tell me a little more about it?" gets the "It's French" or "It's very good" type response. When you query the degree of dryness, the name of the brand, the year, or any other basic piece of information, your "authoritative" waiter, the one with the "red wine" mentality, raises his eyebrows and shrugs his shoulders, wondering why you want such data that seems so pointless—after all, few other diners ask these questions today. In many parts of Europe, thank God, it's different. People do ask.

Few restaurants know how to store wine, let alone have suitable storage space for it. In too many establishments either the wine sits for months at room temperature in those attractive wine racks that lend ambiance, or it nestles downstairs in a too damp, too dry, too cold, or too hot basement—all these extreme conditions being hostile to wine. What the average American restaurateur does to wine is not only deplorable, it should be labeled a culinary crime.

Restaurants also tend to sell wine that hasn't been given enough time to mature because, with a lack of suitable storage space and capital, the owner must turn over his wine stock rapidly. The same is true for most of the wholesalers from whom the restaurants purchase their wines. That wine, you guessed it, isn't yet ready to drink. (For the record, a few—but only a few—liquor stores and restaurants do attempt to give some of their purchased wine sufficient storage time.)

For the sake of argument, let us assume that a perfectly matured bottle of wine is waiting for us in the ideal restaurant cellar. Our problems have not disappeared if the wine has a sediment because most waiters simply go to the cellar, bring the bottle up to the table, and serve it, sediment and all. Even if the bottle were decanted at the table, the shaking and wobbling that the bottle usually goes through on its journey from the cellar to the dining room will have infused the wine with the sediment, and all the king's horses could not make it resettle in less than a few hours; likely longer. The only strategies are to bring the bottle up to the dining room the day before (impractical) or to decant it expertly in the basement (unlikely). What I am suggesting is that ordering a great wine in a restaurant is not only expensive but usually crazy.

Another potential storage faux pas that hits the diner concerns jug wine. Many restaurants simply recap the leftover jug wine and leave it at room temperature for the next meal. If the bottle is partially empty (as it will be), the air inside will turn the wine sour. If you are one of the first customers for dinner or particularly, for lunch, request that your house wine be served from a fresh, unopened bottle.

The use of wine cradles (or baskets) is still another storage-related folly. For a discussion of what wine cradles should do and should not do, see page 76.

An interesting problem I sometimes encounter occurs after I have knowledgeably matched the wine to the dish. I discover, for instance, that chef Jacques's Poulet Chasseur is untraditionally laden with dried fruits or some other iconoclastic surprise. While there is nothing wrong with chef Jacques being creative in the kitchen, he should not call the dish by a misleading name. Let him call it Poulet Chez Moi or, if he is vain, Poulet Jacques—but not Poulet Chasseur.

At times you may be unfamiliar with or unsure of the characteristics of a wine or of the dish. My best advice in these situations is to ask. It has always puzzled me why some knowledgeable diners are afraid to show their ignorance—the subject of wine and food is so vast that after spending some twenty years diligently studying the subject, I still need at least another ten lifetimes to know the answers to even the basic culinary questions.

Ask for the wine list when you are given the menu. Most of the time you'll find yourself choosing the food first, then selecting an appropriate wine, but on occasions you may find a bottle you particularly want to try, so you reverse your match-up process by selecting the food to match the wine. If the wine list is limited, you may be forced to select the wine and the food on a simultaneous basis, choosing on the basis of what is available, appealing, and compatible.

When ordering a red wine, ask the waiter to bring the bottle immediately to your table for two particular reasons. The early arrival and opening of the wine will allow it to breathe (I discuss this concept on page 75). Having the wine brought early will also assure that the wine will be tested, ready, and waiting when your hot plates arrive from the kitchen (few things are more disconcerting in a restaurant than having your entrée just sit there getting cold while a hovering waiter opens the bottle, asks your approval, and then pours the wine).

At times this waiting-for-the-wine syndrome is even worse: The wine bottle is nowhere in sight because your waiter forgot to fetch it. This contemptible oversight is most likely to occur when you've ordered a white wine to accompany your appetizer and/or fish course. To guard against those situations, I try to remember politely to ask the waiter not to bring the appetizer (or fish course) until the white wine has been poured.

When the waiter brings the bottle to the table, examine the label to verify that it is indeed the wine you ordered and not a different bottle because of a substitution or error. Check the name and vintage of the wine along with the name of the importer and shipper. While examining the label, also look at the bottle's neck. Does it show signs of leaking? Does it have an excessive ullage (the air space in the bottle)? Does the cork easily slide down into the bottle when lightly pushed with your finger? All these are bad indicators, for they portend an oxidized, maderized, or just plain sourish wine. If a bottle shows these characteristics, I would ask for another bottle or perhaps even another wine. If the waiter insists that the wine will be agreeable, accept his wisdom, but make it clear that you will reject the bottle if your prediction comes true.

The waiter's next step is to open the bottle. Make sure he performs this task in your presence because there have been instances where a bottle was substituted for one that had been previously opened and rejected at another table—or where the bottle was refilled with a lesser wine.

It is customary for the waiter to show you the cork. Some wine writers think this tradition is meaningless, but I disagree. First, the stamp of the cork of a fine wine will usually substantiate that this is indeed the wine you ordered and not merely a lesser bottle upon which is glued the wine label of your choice. This has happened to me a couple of times, including in one restaurant where an unscrupulous owner soaked off the label of an empty Château Cheval Blanc bottle and glued it over the label of an ordinary Saint-Emilion. Another time the stamped cork and the bottle label were in agreement with the vineyard's name but not with the desired vintage (there's a big difference in price and quality between a 1961 and a 1963 Château Lafite-Rothschild).

Another reason for giving you the cork is to allow you to sniff it, an act that will help you to determine if the wine has turned sourish or corkish (the latter defect is caused by a faulty cork). I really see little purpose in this cork-sniffing ritual because if a wine is off, you will be better able to estimate the degree and type of defect when sniffing the wine once it is poured into the glass.

Sometimes the top of the cork is a little moldy. A small amount of mold that has restricted itself to the top quarter of the cork is, in most instances, not damaging to the wine. Nor is the mold likely to be harmful to your health as long as you do not allow it to reach the wine. This top-of-the-cork mold is usually caused by storing the wine in a damp cellar, which is a lesser sin than storing the wine in a dry cellar, where corks have a tendency to contract and let airborne vinegar bacteria into the bottle.

Wineglasses should already be on the table. If it is a knowledgeable and conscientious restaurant, the glasses will be able to hold at least eight ounces. How sad it is to be given those three- or four-ounce glasses that seem to be everywhere. Restaurants love them because of their low-breakage qualities, but from the customer's point of view, you cannot adequately swirl the wine to release its bouquet. New glasses should be brought out every time a different wine is served.

Even that minute residue of the previous wine that clings to the side of the glass can alter the taste of the new wine, especially if the latter is delicate.

Tradition calls for the waiter to pour a one-inch-or-so portion into the host's glass so that the latter may sample the wine. This ritual also helps assure that the host and not the other diners get the cork bits, should they exist. In centuries past, this custom also helped prove to any suspicious guest that the wine was without poison.

If a man and woman are at the table, virtually every waiter automatically assumes that the taster should be the male and consequently pours the sample wine portion into the man's glass. Is it not possible that in some instances the woman may be a better judge of the wine than the man? If both persons are knowledgeable, why not ask the waiter to pour a little into both glasses, allowing both tablemates to share the fun of judging the wine?

Your eyes, nose, and taste buds should be on the lookout for a number of factors. Questions you should be asking yourself include: Is the wine in sound condition? Is the wine what it is supposed to be? Is the wine at the right serving temperature?

When judging the wine, make sure your palate is properly fresh and cleansed. I've seen too many situations where a diner rejected a bottle because it tasted off, while in fact the sensory reaction was the result of the vinegar-drenched salad, an oily hors d'oeuvre, a spicy tidbit, or some other wine-hostile food that he just ate. If you have just tainted your palate when the waiter asks you to sample the wine, either refresh your palate with a piece of bread or a sip of water—or ask him to come back in a few minutes when your palate will be in better shape to make an intelligent judgment.

If you accept the wine, give the waiter a nod and—if the

wine is remarkably good—articulate your joy. The waiter pours the wine, starting with the person on your left, and proceeds clockwise until he returns to finish filling your glass. By filling, I mean no more than one-half full—and if the glass is a big one, no more than one-third full. This will leave you sufficient room to release the wine's bouquet by swirling the glass.

Some hosts and waiters prefer to serve the female guests first, then the male guests. This protocol seems a little sexist and outdated to me.

After serving a white wine or Champagne, the waiter puts it back into an ice bucket. A few thoughts are in order on this subject. The most common error is leaving the wine too long in the wine cooler, thereby overchilling it and, in the process, numbing your senses and not allowing the wine to release its flavored bouquet sufficiently. Whenever a wine stays too long in the bucket, ask the waiter to dry off the bottle and to stand it on the table for ten or fifteen minutes. Another shortcoming of the wine bucket system is that few models of this equipment are sufficiently deep. What happens is that the bottom half of the wine gets overly chilled while the top half (the portion the waiter pours first) remains relatively warm. When faced with these squat wine buckets, turn the unopened bottle of white wine upside down into the iced water for about ten to fifteen minutes just prior to opening the bottle. The bucket, by the way, should not merely contain ice. A fifty-fifty combination of ice and water offers the quickest cooling qualities. (Tip: Put the water in first, then add the ice cubes; reversing this order causes the ice cubes to freeze together in bunches.)

You have the traditional right to reject a wine at no cost to you—but make sure you have a valid cause. Unfortunately for restaurateurs, most wines are sent back without justifiable reasons. Some are refused because of what the taster previously ate, while others are rejected because the diner was trying to impress himself, his guests, or the restaurant proprietor. Sometimes the diner thinks the wine is off because he has a mistaken belief of how it should taste. Too many diners claim a wine is corky, a defect that seldom happens in real life.

One story that comes to mind occurred at a restaurant where I used to work during my school days. A rather pompous diner rejected a wine out of hand, without being able to articulate the reasons for his displeasure beyond vague claims of it not being drinkable. The owner apologized, took the bottle back to the kitchen, poured it into a carafe, and brought it out saying, "Perhaps you would prefer our carafe wine—it's humble, but it has no defects." The diner took a sip and exclaimed, "Now that's what I call a good wine." I detected a victorious smirk across the face of the proprietor.

When deciding whether to accept or reject a wine, try not to think in black and white terms, as some diners do. Few things in life are in an absolute state of perfection, so be prepared to allow for slight imperfections. Of course, the more money you spend, the smaller your tolerance should be.

On the other side of the coin, there are evenings when the wine is defective and the maître d'hotel either refuses to exchange it or does it in a disdainful manner after having failed in his attempt to intimidate you into accepting it. The worst thing you can do is to let this sticky situation upset you and thereby ruin your dinner. Finish your meal in peace, electing to get even later by not coming back and by bad-mouthing the establishment to your friends, the ultimate revenge.

II
Other Tips and Insights

Buying Wine

More than half the battle of buying wine is over if you have a quality wine merchant in your area. Ideally, both the owner and his staff should be well informed, the result of their intrinsic love of wines in general and of satisfying their intellectual curiosity about the wines they sell. You and I both know that there is a paucity of these ideal stores—so when we find one, we should develop the professional friendship with the personnel for their wine-buying counsel.

Since no single wine store can possibly carry everything, and since sometimes the prices vary on a given bottle from outlet to outlet, I recommend that you do comparison shopping in a number of establishments, providing that each one handles wine knowledgeably (a wine merchant's mistreatment of wine in his hot cellar or window can make any possible glories of a vineyard meaningless).

Generally, the more we pay for a bottle in a given store, the less likely we are to buy a defective wine—that's a well-proven law of shopping. The same is true as we go up the quality scale of Bordeaux vineyards or the Burgundy shippers (for your information, among the best and most reliable of the popular Burgundy negotiants are Drouhin, Louis Jadot, and Louis Latour).

Whenever you're in a store that seems far more of a booze than a wine store in orientation, be chary about following the advice of the clerk, unless his conversation indicates that he really knows something about the wine—and that he himself drinks the wine he is touting. In too many instances the clerk is praising the merits of a particular wine simply because his boss asked him to push it. (The wine could be a high-profit item or one that is overstocked or starting to go downhill.)

Some states—those with "monopoly stores"—will have a limited and usually poor wine selection. There is little we can do except to make the most of their lackluster stock and write a strong letter of protest to our state legislators.

Storing Wine

The advantages of storing wine in your home are multifold and significant: You can take advantage of special sales, you can usually earn a 10 percent discount by buying in case lots, you can save time and headaches by not having to run down to the wine store every time you need a wine, and you will generally have a wide selection of well-rested wines to match your food and mood of the moment.

If you have a quality wine cellar, you derive still other benefits. You can save money because you can buy wines when they first come on the market (as they mature, their prices tend to escalate). You can also enjoy drinking wines at their prime because the expensive red wines offered in the liquor store more often than not need at least a few more years' storage. But don't think of your wine cellar as an investment. Wine prices may suddenly drop (as they did in the early to mid-seventies). And unlike postage stamps and other hobby collections, you can't resell your wine unless you have the required government license.

Your ideal cellar should have storage bins where your bottles can be stored on their sides, label side up for ease of reading as well as for collecting the sediment along one line. Laying the wines horizontally keeps the corks moist and thereby keeps them from drying out. (If your bottles have metal caps rather than corks, it doesn't matter whether you store your wine upright, horizontal, or upside down.) The temperature in your cellar should be approximately 55 degrees Fahrenheit (13 degrees Centigrade) if you want your wine to mature properly. Too low a temperature stunts the vital maturation process, while too high a temperature speeds it up, thereby lessening the resulting quality. Temperature fluctuations, such as 40 degrees F. in winter and 70 degrees F. in summer, also negatively hasten the maturation process—and the more sudden, frequent, and/or extreme these fluctuations, the worse your wine will fare.

Your ideal cellar should also be pitch-dark, as light is harmful to and speeds up the work of the delicate organisms that are helping wine to mature. Vibrations such as those from an underground subway, an elevator shaft, or a banging closet door also disrupt and speed up the chemistry, much to the detriment of your wine. Too damp a storage environment will encourage the formation of mold on the cork, while too dry an environment will cause the cork to dry up and shrink, letting airborne vinegar bacteria into the bottle. Since the cork is porous (as it should be), foul aromas from old hiking boots, decaying vegetables, and the like can sneak into the wine unless we are careful about the wine's storage mates.

But don't fret if you don't have the ideal wine cellar, because few of us do or will ever have one. Your biggest loss is not being able to lay away fine wines over a long stretch of time. For most other wines, the environment provided by a 65- to 72-degree house or apartment living room is seldom hostile for limited time periods. Ordinary wine can be stored up to four to six months, good wines can be safely stored for two or three months, and great wines are reasonably safe for up to a month. This implies, of course, that potentially harmful factors such as temperature fluctuations and vibrations are kept to a minimum—and that factors like direct sunlight are absent. If the wine is stored in a quiet closet rather than being displayed in a decorator wine rack in the living room, so much the better.

When storing wines, remember that white wines generally need a slightly cooler temperature than red wines, so store the whites on the bottom of your wine rack (the air temperature near the floor is about five degrees cooler than that near the ceiling because, as we learned in our science classes, hot air rises and cold air sinks). But if your reds are far better in quality than your whites, I would give the location preference to the more precious reds.

Vintages

Unless you are very dedicated to the subject of wine, I would suggest you forget about trying to memorize the vintage ratings and just carry in your wallet or purse one of the pocket-sized vintage cards supplied free by most wine merchants.

Besides, we as Americans tend to fix into our heads that a certain year was good or bad without knowing all the many exceptions to the rules that make vintage charts no more than crude maps of a complex territory. Certainly, to any explorer a map of that quality would be better than none at all, but no explorer who values his life would overly rely upon the map.

The exceptions to the rules that I have referred to take

many forms. First, there has never been a bad year when some nearby and possible contiguous vineyards didn't produce a good wine. The reverse is true, too. Second, while a 1970 Château Lafite-Rothschild promises to be a better wine than a 1967 bottle, the latter will be more enjoyable to drink until the slower maturing 1970 wine reaches a reasonable point of maturity, which probably won't take place until the early 1980s—or perhaps even later. Third, the smaller the bottle of a given wine, the faster it will mature—figure on a half bottle maturing 15 to 20 percent faster than a regular-sized bottle, which in turn will probably mature 10 to 15 percent faster than a magnum or double-sized bottle. Fourth, a bottle of wine that has undergone mistreatment in terms of transportation or storage will reach its peak sooner, though the quality of the wine will be only a shadow of the glory that wine would have attained if properly handled. Fifth, some of the vintages printed on the labels of certain inexpensive imported wines are pure fiction.

Even if you don't have a vintage card, I wouldn't be that concerned because with most of the wines we buy, it's not the reputation of the vintage year that counts most, it's the absolute age of the wine. With most whites and practically all rosés, for instance, we want to be on guard against buying too old a bottle because the contents may have lost its freshness and begun to sour. For the more expensive wines—especially the reds—we can usually ascertain the most highly touted (but not necessarily the best) years by their price tags.

Wine Quantity per Person

While determining how much wine to serve a group of people is an estimate at best, I can give you a few guidelines to make your job easier.

The first order of business is to know how many servings you can pour out of a bottle. A standard-sized bottle (three-quarters of a liter, or 25.4 ounces) contains a fraction more than six four-ounce portions, the perfect amount for an eight- to twelve-ounce wineglass.

Your next task is to analyze the occasion. Americans usually drink far more wine at dinner than at lunch. They also increase their consumption as the size of the group increases because of the conviviality factor. Wine drinking also tends to increase in proportion to the length of the event— those organized gourmet dinners that go on for three to five hours usually call for a full bottle (or two) per person. Gaiety also increases booze consumption, as most wedding receptions verify. The drinking habits of the individual guest must also be taken into consideration. Some people are satisfied with a single glass, while for others, a full bottle per meal is normal. Finally, as people increase their intake of predinner cocktails, their desire for wine during the meal will probably decrease.

Generally, you can figure on one glass of wine for a light meal, two for an ordinary meal, and three for a special dinner—but plug into your mental computer those variables I've mentioned in the preceding paragraph.

Whatever your estimate, it is wiser to overestimate than to underestimate the quantity, as you can probably use the leftover wine the following day (see pages 79–80 for more details).

Wineglasses

When served in quality glasses, great wines always taste better, good wines almost always taste better, and ordinary wines often taste better. Few experienced wine drinkers would disagree with this contention.

Fortunately, we no longer have to spend a small fortune for quality glasses. Though those hand-blown twenty-five-dollar masterpieces produced by such illustrious firms as Baccarat are worth every penny for anyone with a good income and a love of wine, if you are on a budget and shop wisely, you need not spend over four or five dollars for a reasonably decent glass, thanks to today's manufacturing processes.

Another saving for us is that it is no longer socially *de rigueur* to have a suite of different glasses that correspond to different regional table wines, be they Moselle, Burgundy, Bordeaux, or Chianti. All you need are two sets of all-purpose glasses: One relatively inexpensive set for ordinary meals and a slightly larger-sized and better quality set for special occasions, so long as both these sets (and especially the better one) meet the various specifications that I have outlined below.

A good all-purpose wineglass should be made of thin, colorless glass (preferably lead crystal) without etchings or other markings that may impair your visual judgment of the wine.

Your all-purpose wineglass should have a capacity somewhere between eight to twelve ounces, approximately the size of a large California navel orange. If the bowl is too small, you won't be able to release—via a gentle swirling motion—the bouquet of a four-ounce portion of wine. Those oversized twenty-ounce glasses make more sense as conversation pieces than as practicalities. Not only are they a headache to wash but the wine's bouquet tends to get slightly rarefied within the super bowl.

The bowl shape of your all-purpose wineglass should be bulbous, or, if you prefer, one approximating a tulip. In both cases the top of the bowl should be tapered slightly inward in order to concentrate and capture the wine's bouquet. There should not be a noticeable lip on the rim of the bowl (a bulging lip is favored in restaurants because it reduces breakage).

Finally, the all-purpose wineglass should have a plain,

three- to four-inch stem, long enough for a large man's fingers to grip it comfortably. The stem's chief purpose as far as wine drinking is concerned is to prevent the drinker's hands from smudging the bowl and from warming the wine. As for holding the glass and swirling the wine, these feats could be done equally as adroitly with or without the stem.

After you have purchased your ordinary and special-occasion sets of all-purpose glasses, your next set will largely depend on your wine-drinking habits. Most people take the step toward Champagne glasses because sparkling wines are fun to serve at home. Whatever you do, don't purchase those saucer-shaped coupé glasses which are more suitable for puddings and ice-cream sundaes than for Champagne because their extensive open service hastens the escape of the bubbles, turning the wine flat. Your best choice are the long-stemmed, elongated tulip-shaped glasses with a small, concentrated bottom which serves to prolong the effervescent life of Champagne by slowing down the release of the carbon dioxide bubbles. Other possible sets to investigate are one for Cognac or brandy (buy a short-stemmed, six- to eight-ounce snifter), and one for sherry (purchase a short-stemmed, four-ounce somewhat tulip-shaped glass).

The Rhine- or Moselle-style glasses are not really necessary unless you are an avid German wine fancier. If you buy those glasses, stay away from the ones with colored or frosted stems, as that custom developed centuries ago when some German wines had the habit of becoming cloudy. With improved viticultural techniques, this defect is all but gone, so the unclear stems serve no purpose other than to keep you from appreciating the clarity of today's wine. While on the subject of stems, let me advise you against buying any glass with a hollow stem—they are difficult to clean and may even create a health problem if you don't thoroughly wash, rinse, and dry them.

When you have more than one set of wineglasses, you can add charm to your dinner by setting the table with different glasses, each one for a separate wine. It is the usual procedure to serve the white wine in the smaller glass and the red in the larger glass. If two reds (or whites) are being served, pour the better one into the higher quality and/or larger glass. Having two distinct glasses also helps prevent the diner from forgetting which wine is in which glass.

Your ordinary wineglass can be washed just like your everyday water glasses; just treat the former with a little more care. Your better wineglasses—the ones you reserve for special dinners and fine wines—should be washed only in a small amount of mild soap or detergent, and thoroughly rinsed at least half a dozen times. Even better, use plain hot water instead of soap or detergent because these two substances can alter the flavor of a delicate wine and, in the case of Champagne, can somewhat impede the beautiful release of the bubbles (slowing down the carbon dioxide release rate is desirable, but not in this manner). When washed, dry and polish your fine glasses with dirt-, soap-, lint- and aroma-free cloth until the glass is spotless and sparkles all over when held up to the light.

Store your glasses right side up. Putting them in your storage space upside down, as many people do, will encourage the inside of the wineglass to pick up the odor from the shelving. If wineglasses have been stored for a long time in between uses, rewash and polish them to get rid of any odor or dust they may have picked up.

Table Setting

While there is no single socially correct table setting, all the widely accepted variations have one trait in common: functionalism. Thus, the salad fork is served on the outside of the dinner fork if the salad is to be eaten first—and, by the same logic, the soup spoon is usually placed outside the dessert spoon (unless the latter is placed horizontally above the plate). The water glass is served on the right side (in circle A in my diagram, just above the knife) because nearly 90 percent of the human race is right-handed. If a wine but no water is to be served, as is the custom in France, the wineglass is placed in circle A. If both water and wine are to be served, as is popular in America, the water is allocated circle A and the wine, circle B, to the right and slightly below circle A. If a white wine is to be served prior to a red wine, its glass is placed in circle C (since the red won't be poured until the white wineglass is removed from the table, it is not obstructed).

Wine Serving Temperature

I find that the majority of American restaurants and homes tend to serve red wines too warm while overchilling their white ones. The principal reason for overwarming the reds is that people blindly follow the "serve reds at room temperature" dictum. That rule was formulated by Europeans of past centuries, whose dining rooms were typically heated in the 65- to 68-degree zone, sometimes lower. Modern-day American homes and dining establishments are customarily heated to about 72 degrees—and not infrequently up to 80 degrees. White wines are overchilled because people leave the wine too long in the refrigerator or wine bucket.

Virtually all still red table wines are best served between 55 and 68 degrees Fahrenheit (13 to 20 degrees Centigrade). Generally, the better, the fuller bodied, and/or the drier the red wine is, the closer to 68 degrees you should come because you want this type of wine to give forth all the subtle aromas and flavors it possesses. To illustrate, a great Médoc should be served at 68 degrees, while most jug reds—which have few nuances to lose—are best at about 55 degrees, a temperature that is refreshing to the palate as far as red wines are concerned. The lower temperature also helps mask a wine's defects.

White (and rosé) wines are best enjoyed somewhere between 45 degrees and 55 degrees Fahrenheit (7 to 13 degrees Centigrade). Again, the better, the fuller bodied, and/or the drier the wine, the closer you should come to the maximum temperature, 55 degrees. Thus, serve an unhyphenated Montrachet at 55 degrees but an ordinary jug white at about 45 degrees.

The temperature zone for Champagne and dessert wines is 40 to 50 degrees Fahrenheit (4 to 10 degrees Centigrade). The sweeter the wine, the colder the temperature should generally be. A brut Champagne is best at around 50 degrees, while a sweet Champagne comes off best at around 40 degrees. Since dessert wines are sweet by their very nature, serve them hovering around 40 degrees. The exceptions to the rule are those great lusciously sweet wines like the Trockenbeerenauslese and the best of the French Sauternes—serve them around 55 degrees, lest you numb some of their subtle qualities.

Chilling the Wine

Exactly what is 65 or 68 degrees Fahrenheit? About the only real way to know is to make firsthand experiments: Measure the temperature of wines at various degree levels, then taste these wines until you can recognize the various temperature levels. An excellent instrument for this task is the Taylor instant thermometer (retails for about twelve dollars). Until you develop this temperature-perception expertise, I am afraid you'll just have to make rough guesses.

You have two basic ways to chill a white, rosé, or sparkling wine: the refrigerator and the wine bucket method. Avoid placing a wine in the freezer—this procedure shocks the wine and runs the risk of an exploding bottle should you forget to remove it within a few hours. Instead, plan well ahead and place the bottle in the warmest area of a refrigerator (low to medium thermostat setting). Assuming that the bottle is starting off at a typical room temperature of 72 degrees I suggest that you refrigerate the wine for approximately half an hour to bring it down to 60 degrees, one hour to 50 degrees, and two hours to 40 degrees. Since all refrigerators are different, adjust these time periods after you make a few experiments.

With the ice bucket method, reduce the time for the refrigerator method by two-thirds (one hour by this formula becomes twenty minutes). The precise time will vary according to the depth and diameter of the bucket, the ice-to-water ratio (ideally 1:1), the initial temperature, and whether you turned the unopened bottle upside down. For additional discussion on wine buckets, see page 57.

If you want to reduce the temperature of a fine red from 72

to 68 degrees, the sudden temperature changes of the refrigerator or ice bucket methods will harm it. To lower the wine to 68 degrees, rest the bottle in a sufficiently large plastic bag (to keep the label dry) and submerge it in a large container of 60-degree water for about one hour.

Opening a Bottle

I have seen and tried about a hundred different types of corkscrews. Each one has its devoted adherents who argue that it is simply the best in the world and that everyone should own one. The selection of a corkscrew, like an automobile, is largely—except for the price tag factor—a matter of mission and personal preference. The best of the readily available corkscrews are, I believe, the ones with leverage-type mechanisms because they gently ease the cork from the bottle. Examples of this type are the double-action bolt and the twin-armed butterfly corkscrews. The traditional waiter's corkscrew also works on the leverage principle, but to learn how to use it without jerking the cork or bottle requires a lot of practice. Besides, the primary reason waiters prefer their traditional corkscrew is because this self-contained implement, with knife and all, fits snugly into a tuxedo pocket, without any bulk. The old-fashioned and usually inexpensive T-shaped opener is one of the worst varieties; it demands quite a bit of pulling and tugging, a potentially dangerous exercise because, among other hazards, you might break the bottle.

The type of worm (or screw) is important. The ideal worm has—on its lengthwise axis—a hollow spiral, one into which you can insert a wooden match. The threads should be relatively smooth rather than cork-cutting sharp. Because you frequently encounter long corks, especially when it comes to better Bordeaux wines, the worm should be at least two inches long.

Your first bottle-opening step is to remove the metallic foil or capsule by cutting it just below the lip of the bottle with the sharp point of a small knife. With a clean cloth, wipe the bottle lip and top of the cork to remove any mold or other foreign matter that might come into contact with the wine. Insert the corkscrew and gently remove the cork. Again wipe the bottle lip, being careful not to let any substances fall into the wine.

If a cork should break (something that will eventually happen to you if you open enough bottles), you can filter out the minute fragments through a fine plastic sieve or through a cheesecloth drooped over a nonmetallic funnel. A coffee filter will also work, but I would not suggest it for a good wine, as the superefficient filter will collect some of the flavor as well as the cork bits. I really don't recommend your buying those gimmicky multipronged cork retrievers as they do little more than remove the large cork chunks, a task you could do in any number of other obvious ways. What we are after are those small cork remnants.

Opening a bottle of Champagne is an entirely different operation. The most important goal in uncorking a Champagne bottle is to minimize the popping sound. While such noise adds Hollywood-type festivity to the occasion, it is caused by the gas escaping from the Champagne, something we would like to prevent unless—Bacchus save us—we prefer our beverage on the flat side. To reduce the internal pressure and thereby the sound, have the bottle well rested (over a period of at least twenty-four hours) and properly chilled before attempting to open it. Wrap the bottle in a napkin, placing both in your left hand if you are right-handed. The bottle should be pointing upward at an angle of 45 degrees to reduce the pressure that the gas exerts against the cork. The bottle should also be pointing away from anything breakable or breathing, as the cork can become a miniature cannonball, a lethal weapon. With your right hand, remove the metallic foil, then untwist and set aside the metal muzzle, being careful that the cork doesn't prematurely eject.

Grasp the cork firmly in your right hand and twist the bottle (not the cork, whose top can break off). Keep twisting the bottle until the cork comes free, but all the time—and especially during the last few seconds—keeping a firm downward pressure on the cork to slow down its emergence. Success is when you barely hear the pop.

Letting a Wine Breathe

Red wines usually need about a half hour to three hours to breathe. Generally, the more tannin in a wine, the more breathing time it requires. Some fine old wines at their peak—and therefore with their tannin content reduced with time—need only fifteen to thirty minutes, just long enough to let the mustiness out of the wine (you would be musty, too, if you spent many years in a bottle). If left to breathe longer, the wines could start going downhill, losing much of whatever virtues they had to offer. Other wines, like some undervalued Italian Barolos or Rhône Côte Rôties sometimes need several hours or more. One wine I sampled required twelve hours, and I have heard of wines needing even more time.

Most of the modest, inexpensive reds that we find on today's market really don't need more than thirty to sixty minutes' breathing time because those wines don't have that high a tannic content. I'm speaking of wines like ordinary Burgundies and modern-day mass-market Côtes-du-Rhône.

White and rosé wines need only a few minutes' breathing time, just long enough to let out their bottle-caused mustiness.

The Wine Cradle/Basket

Of the many functionally nonsensical customs in wine drinking, the wine cradle deserves to be nominated for the top spot. Its original and only practical value is to help transport a sediment-laden bottle from the cellar rack to the decanting table. The cradle keeps the bottle horizontal and the label facing upward—and minimizes any tilting, twisting, or shaking the wine is sure to experience on its little journey. To place the wine in a cradle after it has been mishandled is closing the proverbial barn door after the horse has escaped.

Those attractive wicker or straw wine cradles are okay if you take them for what they are: decorative ornaments that lend atmosphere. If the wine has no sediment, go ahead and use one if it pleases you—no harm will be done except to the ulcer of a finicky gourmet. On the other hand, if your wine has thrown a sediment deposit, decant the wine and forget about using the wine basket, otherwise the back and forth sloshing movement that the wine will undergo during the pouring process will surely blend the desirable wine with the unwanted sediment.

Decanting

We decant wine to separate the liquid from any sediment that the wine may have thrown during its maturation period. Though this sediment is harmless from a medical point of view, it will cloud as well as distort the overall flavor of the wine.

Except in extremely rare cases, there is no need to decant a white or rosé wine. Nor will you probably have to decant red wines under five years of age because it is very unlikely that they will have thrown a sediment.

Before commencing with the decanting operation, you must stand the bottle up so that the sediment slowly settles to the bottom of the bottle. Many wine writers say that one or two hours is usually ample time for the deposit to sink, but my own carefully controlled experiments have proven that it takes at least three or four hours and, with a fine old wine, twenty-four hours. In the latter case, perhaps forty-eight hours is even better because it gives the sediment substance a better chance to coagulate, thereby minimizing the quantity of wasted undecanted wine that remains in the bottle. A better but more delicate alternative to standing the bottle of wine up is to decant the bottle immediately after taking it from the wine rack, being careful to keep the bottle horizontal and label side up at all times.

When opening a bottle you wish to decant, remove all the foil to ensure that you have maximum visibility through the entire neck of the bottle. Your decanting goal is to transfer the wine in the bottle to another container, usually a decorative decanter, sometimes a plain carafe. Pick up the bottle with a firm grip and, in one continuous motion, slowly pour the wine into the wide-necked decanter, being careful not to stir up the sediment by sloshing the wine back and forth. If possible, have the wine slide down the side of the decanter instead of splashing onto the decanter's bottom. Stop pouring immediately when you first detect some of the sediment appearing in the neck of the bottle. To facilitate your seeing this sediment, place a candle, electric light, or flashlight several inches behind and below the neck of the bottle. Another alternative, if you have a steady and practiced pair of hands, is to decant while holding the two vessels up to a ceiling light. If the bottle is not overly opaque, you really don't need a special light, as a brightly lit white background surface will do nicely.

With most fine old red wines, you will leave behind in the bottle 5 to 10 percent of their original content, depending on the specific wine and your decanting expertise. This one- or two-ounce loss is a worthwhile sacrifice considering that the remaining 90 to 95 percent of the wine will be much more pleasant to drink.

What should you do with the sediment residual? Throw it away, as it is unpleasantly bitter. I've seen several food and wine books that recommend that you save the residual for sauces, but I am afraid the writers were either not good cooks or did not test their advice prior to putting it down on paper for the "benefit" of their readers.

Even if you don't have to do it for the sake of the wine, decanting is an innocent enough exercise that provides you the opportunity of using your glittering crystal decanter at the dining table. And because of the aeration effect of a wine passing from one vessel to another and because the decanter gives the wine a larger top surface, the decanting operation reduces the breathing time needed.

Pouring the Wine

In a restaurant it is customary to serve the host's glass first, but this is senseless at home because, presumably, the host has—or should have—already tasted and personally approved the wine (as well as removed any bits of cork) in his or her kitchen or dining room prior to sitting down to the meal. Yet, many Americans love going through the motions of this table ritual in order either to impress the guests (a negative) or to add a little glamor to the occasion (fine, if the host doesn't take himself or the procedure seriously).

Since there is no need to give the host a sample portion, the serving begins on the host's left and proceeds clockwise, ending with the host. As I said before, to serve the ladies first seems to me an outdated and sexist custom. On very informal occasions, simply let each guest pour—or at least refill—his glass at his own bidding.

At table gatherings exceeding half a dozen persons, two bottles of the same wine will likely be required. Place one near the host and the second at the other end of the table.

If the wine has been decanted, put the empty bottle on the table near the decanter so your guests will readily know what wine they are drinking. I consider it a gross breach of good manners to force a guest against his or her will to guess the wine and its credentials.

As the wine is being poured, the wineglasses remain untouched on the table. Each glass should be filled to roughly one-third capacity, and definitely no more than half filled. A quick, clockwise sixth-of-a-turn twist of the server's wrist helps prevent drops from spilling on the tablecloth (if red wine spillage does occur, immediately pour salt or white wine on the stained area).

Whatever the serving procedure, the wine is always poured before the accompanying food is served. This prevents the food from cooling unnecessarily.

What to Do with Leftover Wine

Because it is difficult to estimate accurately how much wine will be needed for a given dinner and because it's a poor host who lets a wine supply run out before a dinner's end, one is more than occasionally faced with an age-old problem: What to do with leftover wines.

The staying power of a leftover wine is principally contingent upon a combination of several variables: air supply, temperature, and wine type.

Fresh air bears vinegar bacteria, those dastardly fellows who change a perfectly delightful wine into an undrinkable sourish liquid. As soon as you know you're not going to drink any more of the wine, recork the bottle immediately.

Ullage—or the air space between the bottom of the cork

and the top of the wine—makes a difference too. The more ullage, the more air there is inside the wine to cause the wine to turn sour. Should your wine bottle be only half full, transfer its contents to a clean, half-bottle-sized container, thereby eliminating excessive ullage.

With the exceptions mentioned in the next paragraph, recorked wine should be stored in the refrigerator because the lower temperature will slow the development of the vinegar bacteria. Storing it at about 40 to 45 degrees Fahrenheit (4 to 7 degrees Centigrade), the most likely temperature reading of the warmest part of your refrigerator, is probably the best level. If the temperature is any lower than that your wine will suffer more short-term damage from Old Man Frost than from bacteria.

An alternative to refrigerating your good wines is to put them in airtight bottles filled to the point where virtually no ullage exists. Store these bottles in a dark, cool (50 to 60 degrees Fahrenheit or 10 to 16 degrees Centigrade) cellar or cabinet. They will probably fight off the vinegar attack no better than their refrigerated brethren, but at least the chill of the refrigerator won't destroy their delicate qualities as much.

Certain types of wine have longer staying power than others. The drier a wine, the better its quality, and/or the lower its alcoholic content, the shorter the wine's storage lifetime will likely be. With a fine red wine, you've wasted practically all its subtle nuances if you try to keep it for the next day, or even for several hours until the next meal. With lesser reds and most whites, one day's—and sometimes up to several days'—storage in refrigeration will do some harm, but not enough to cry over. Sweet and/or fortified wines have the longest storage life-span of all: two weeks, sometimes three—but don't expect these wines to be their former selves.

Sometimes the leftover wine gets a wee bit sourish, not enough to preclude drinking it but to a sufficient degree where you may not thoroughly enjoy it. Rather than throwing this wine away—or keeping it in storage, which is guaranteed to turn it eventually into a very sourish beverage—you can use it to make a punchlike mulled wine in the winter or Sangria in the warmer months. Or you can use it in cooking or as part of a marinade. Still another possibility is to use your leftover wine as a base for wine vinegar, should you have a good mother of vinegar. Commercial bottled vinegars are generally not suitable as mother of vinegar starters because they are usually pasteurized—and even if they were unpasteurized, the quality of their mother of vinegar is seldom inspiring.

Toasting

Giving a congenial toast—or making a witty remark about wine—can add enjoyment to any special-occasion meal. In case you should ever be in need of one, let me share with you some of my favorite toasts:

- "May our friendship, like good wine, improve with age."—old English proverb
- "Eat, drink, and be merry, for tomorrow you must diet."
- "Let's drink a toast to our wine because, as William Shakespeare said, 'Kings it makes gods, and lesser creatures kings.' "
- "I drink to the general joy of the whole table."—William Shakespeare
- "Let us toast the fools, for without them we could not succeed."—Mark Twain
- The one-worder in England and America is, "cheers." Its equivalents in some other parts of the world are:

Kampai (Japan)
Prosit (Germany)
Salud (Spain)
Salute (Italy)
Santé (France)
Skål (Denmark)
Yum-Shing (China)

When wining, dining, and loving, here are a few relevant quotes:

- "A Book of Verses underneath the Bough, a Jug of Wine, a Loaf of Bread—and Thou beside me singing in the Wilderness."—Omar Khayyám
- "It warms the blood, adds luster to the eyes—wine and love have always been allies."—Ovid
- "Drink to me only with thine eyes, and I will pledge with mine; or leave a kiss but in the cup and I'll not look for wine."—Ben Jonson
- "In water one sees one's own face; but in wine one beholds the heart of another."—old French proverb
- "Where there is no wine, there is no love."—Euripedes

And here are a few general sayings that may come in handy at your next dinner party:

- "There is a devil in every berry of the grape."—the Koran
- "A man who was fond of wine was offered some grapes after dinner. 'Much obliged,' he said, pushing the plate to one side, 'I am not accustomed to taking my wine in pills.' "—Brillat-Savarin
- "This wine [said of Montrachet] should be drunk barehead upon one's knees."—Voltaire
- "Never think of leaving perfume or wines to your heir. Administer these yourself and let him have the money."—Martial

- "If God forbade drinking, would he have made wine so good?"—Cardinal Richelieu
- "A bottle of good wine, like a good act, shines ever in the retrospect."—Robert Louis Stevenson
- "It's a simple native American burgundy without any breeding, but I think you'll be amazed by its presumption."—James Thurber

III

Encyclopedia of Foods and International Dishes

This encyclopedia is a quick reference tool to help you find a suitable wine for a particular dish.

For your convenience, this encyclopedia works in reverse to the standard wine book approach, which gives you the name of a wine, then a dish to go with that wine, if the book does so at all. In the vast majority of cases, however, this is not the practical way to solve the problem. Your task is usually to select a wine for a particular dish and not the other way around. I have organized this encyclopedia to allow you to find the food first, then the wine—a sequence that seems to make the most sense.

While this encyclopedia gives you specific suggestions for most of the dishes that you will encounter in restaurants and at home, you will be coming across specialties that are unlisted. This is to be expected, since the number of distinct dishes in this world is virtually infinite. Even to limit myself to the ten thousand or so dishes of which I am personally aware, I would need several colossal volumes, a course of action that is obviously beyond the realistic scope and space availability of my wine-food affinity guidebook.

However, should your dish not be in my encyclopedia,

chances are you will be able to make a knowledgeable decision by following the guidelines set forth in Part I, "Wine
Selection Factors." You will perhaps find additional advice '
under one of this encyclopedia's general entries, which
include:

- Beef
- Cheese
- Chicken
- Desserts
- Duck and Goose
- Eggs
- Fish
- Game
- Ham
- Lamb
- Nuts
- Pasta
- Pork
- Shellfish
- Soup
- Turkey
- Veal
- Vegetables

You will notice that I sometimes recommend no wine
and/or suggest another beverage such as beer. Contrary to
what some wine snobs would have us believe, wine is not
necessarily the only or best alcoholic beverage alternative.

I have also advocated in appropriate circumstances the use
of *vin ordinaire*, the inexpensive but drinkable everyday
wine of America, France, and other countries. It is interesting to note that I have never found a genuine wine connois-
seur who does not enjoy a *vin ordinaire* in the right situation;
at the same time, most of the wine snobs that I know pooh-
pooh these everyday wines.

When it comes to specific wines, I have tried to minimize giving you the names of obscure regional wines that have limited availability in America—to list them would be academic.

Please rest assured that every recommendation has been personally tested and proven by both me and other serious cuisine buffs—so you can follow these suggestions with full confidence. Nevertheless, since most dishes are never prepared or served exactly the same way twice, you would be wise to modify my suggestions in accordance with the guidelines offered in Part I. (Incidentally, with so many possible recipes for each given dish, I have selected the wines based upon a well-researched consensus of authoritative recipes.)

I hope you will feel free to annotate the entries with the name of a wine whenever you discover an affinity that particularly pleases you. For instance, should you find that Château X goes admirably with Veal Piccata, I encourage you to mark it in this book as a permanent reminder for your future enjoyment. You won't be hurting my professional pride because, as I said before, there is never a single right answer—only a large number of wrong match-ups. To list all possible wine alternatives would take thousands upon thousands of pages, thus making this book nonfunctional.

As you gradually increase your affinity knowledge, you will find yourself experimenting more by throwing certain rules out the window (at least temporarily) and following your instincts underpinned by common sense. This is all well and good—after all, a meal should be an enjoyable and adventurous experience and not a rigid exercise following someone else's rules. *Bon appétit.*

Angels on Horseback   The smoky flavor of the bacon in this popular oyster-featured hors d'oeuvre, or savory, as the case may be, is too much for a wine. A fortified wine such as a dry sherry or dry vermouth fares better.

Appenzeller A fair- to good-quality Hermitage, Côte Rôtie, Châteauneuf-du-Pape, Chianti, Rioja, Zinfandel, and other similar assertive, somewhat fruity medium- to full-bodied reds pair well with this cheese. Best national match-up: the red Swiss Dole. Nonwine alternatives: a quality lager beer, ale, or hard cider. *Also see* Cheese.

Apple Providing that the apple is ripe and mild (as opposed to the tart varieties), you can serve a sweet dessert wine like a Sauternes or Barsac, a sweet Champagne, a sweet fortified wine, hard cider, or an apple brandy such as Calvados or Applejack. Avoid serving a mediocre wine with an apple, as the latter will magnify the former's defects.

Apricot Besides apricot brandies, a fine French Sauternes, Hungarian five-*puttonyos* Tokay, or a German Beeren-auslese team well with this stone-pit orchard fruit.

Arroz con Pollo This is basically the "chicken only" version of Paella *(see)*.

Artichoke Table or sparkling wines do not fare well with artichokes in any form: whole or bottoms, stuffed or plain. This is especially true with the popular Artichoke Vinaigrette specialty, as the acid in the marinade sauce compounds the taste distortion. If you want an accompaniment, a fortified wine such as a dry sherry or a dry vermouth will work best.

Avgolemono Soup The substantial egg yolks and lemon juice argue for no wine. Enjoy this Greek soup by itself. *Also see* Soup.

Avocado This fruit does little for table wines, but a good dry white vermouth (especially a Chambéry) or a dry sherry or Madeira make adequate companions, even if the avocado is lightly dressed with a sauce like vinaigrette or mayonnaise, as is the case with the classic Latin American dish of shrimp or crab meat served with avocado and a remoulade or Russian dressing. But if the sauce is very spicy and oniony—as is called for in a Guacamole recipe, switch to a lager beer or ale.

Baba au Rhum   Since the rum flavoring is so pronounced, this dessert tastes better when accompanied by a compatible liqueur, such as Grand Marnier or, even better, a sweet, medium-grade fortified wine such as Marsala.

Baba Ghanouj   A coarse, Mediterranean-style white or rosé, such as one from France's Provence, if not too sweet, is an adequate choice for this Middle Eastern eggplant preparation. A fine or delicate wine would be wasted because of the high lemon content in the dish.

Bacalao à la Vizcaina   A lager beer or ale is best for this Iberian salt cod specialty. If a wine is desired, choose an inexpensive, robust white like a Vinho Verde or Frascati—or a medium-grade white Riosa. Another alternative is a light-bodied red high in acidity, such as a Chinon.

Baked Alaska   The ice cream in this showman's dish precludes serving a fine wine. A liqueur would be best, though a moderately priced sweet sparkling white wine would also serve your purpose.

Baklava   This honey-drenched Greek pastry is too rich to suit any wine. Even a liqueur neither gives nor receives anything of value when partnered with baklava.

Banana   Wine and this fruit fight each other rather viciously. If you are serving it as a dessert, whether with or without sugar or honey, you may want to drink one of the banana liqueurs.

Barbecued Beef The charcoal smoke that permeates the meat is too assertive in flavor and aroma to do any fine wine justice. When barbecueing a good roast or steak, select a medium-priced, full-bodied red such as an average California Cabernet Sauvignon or slightly better than average California Zinfandel. A medium-priced Chianti also works well. If a barbecue sauce teeming with onions, tomatoes, and sugar is used, serve an inexpensive California red jug wine, beer, or ale.

Barbecued Chicken This popular preparation is too robust for anything better than an average red wine, such as a young California Zinfandel, Côtes-du-Rhône, or commonplace Chianti. Also don't forget lager beer or ale.

Barbecued Spareribs Wine doesn't go with this fatty, sweet, and usually sour preparation, a favorite in Chinese restaurants and backyard barbecues; a beer or ale works best. If a wine is to be served, you are best off selecting a modest sparkling red wine, or a rosé with some acidity.

Bavarian Cream A top-grade demi-sec or doux Champagne with enough character to stand up to the cream and egg contents is in order for this rich yet delicate dessert. A fine, sweet fortified wine, such as a Malmsey Madeira, is an alternative choice.

Beaumont This soft, French Savoy cheese is complemented by a parish-level Côte de Nuits Burgundy (such as Nuits-Saint-Georges or Gevrey-Chambertin), Saint-Emilion, Pomerol, Hermitage, Côte Rôtie, Châteauneuf-du-Pape,

California Pinot Noir, or similar full-bodied red. *Also see* Cheese.

Beef As I discussed on pages 8 to 15, the selection of the wine depends on the cooking method, sauce, seasoning, and garnish, among other influences. With beef, it also very much depends on such factors as the quality of the individual animal (the finer the specimen, the better the wine), the age of the animal (the older the creature, the fuller and less delicate the wine), the cut of the beef (the more tender the piece, the better and more subtle the wine), the aging of the beef (the more it has undergone this tenderizing and flavor-enhancing process, the fuller and more assertive the wine), the degree of doneness (the rarer the beef, the fuller the wine), and the serving temperature of the meat (the colder the meat, the more robust the wine). Should you have a very fine red wine, such as a La Tâche, and wish to serve beef, select one of the best cuts and roast or grill it rare and as simply as possible. In respect to your fine wine, I wouldn't barbecue the meat over coals because the charcoal smokiness permeating the meat is much too assertive, both in flavor and in aroma.

You will find suggestions for over fifty of the more popular meat dishes under their individual entries: Roast Beef, Steak au Poivre, and the like.

Beef alla Pizzaiola Serve a young, robust red, such as a Barbera, but nothing better, lest the seasonings overpower the wine.

Beef à la Bourguignonne Serve the same wine used to make this famous French stew. Usually, the chosen wine is a medium-bodied, not too expensive, red southern Burgundy, such as a Santenay. For a domestic alternative, consider a California Pinot Noir.

Beef Stroganoff A medium-grade southern red Burgundy, such as Chalonnais on the order of a Givry or Mercurey, usually fits this dish to a tee. If the dish is superbly made, you may move up to a Beaune, Pommard, or Volnay. A domestic alternative is a medium-grade California Petit Sirah.

Beef Wellington A medium- to fine-grade Hermitage, Côte Rôtie, or Châteauneuf-du-Pape are good choices.

Beer Cheese/Bierkäse A lager beer or ale would do better than a wine, naturally. *Also see* Cheese.

Bel Paese Barolo, Gattinara, Chianti Classico, Chianti, Brunello di Montalcino, Barbaresco, and similar full-bodied reds are suggested for this northern Italian cheese. *Also see* Cheese.

Berries If the berries are in season as well as being fully fresh and ripe (and thus not tart), you have at least several good options: a sweet white dessert wine, such as a French Sauternes or Montbazillac; a sweet fortified wine (Madeira, Porto, and so on); a sweet Champagne. For specific brandy or liqueur match-ups, *see* the following entries: Blackberries, Blueberries, Raspberries, Strawberries.

Billi-bi This rich, creamy oyster soup-stew is good enough to demand a *Premier* or *Grand Cru* Côte d'Or, such as a Bâtard-Montrachet, or one of the finer examples of the California Chardonnays. *Also see* Shellfish.

Bird's Nest Soup No wine is suitable for this classic South China Sea soup (*see* Soup). If one is desired, drink a dry fortified wine such as a Madeira or the Chinese rice "wine," *Shaohsing.*

Biryani Because of its typical robust, well-seasoned flavor, lager beer or ale is generally the best choice for this Middle Eastern and Indian rice dish.

Bisque *See* Soup, and particularly the discussion on cream soups.

Black Bean Soup If thickly made, this soup can be accompanied by the same type of wine (usually a dry sherry) that went into its preparation. If the soup has been thinly prepared, forgo wines altogether (*see* Soup).

Blackberries In addition to the wines mentioned in the Berries entry, you can pair this fruit with a blackberry liqueur.

Blanquette de Veau The rich, creamy sauce for this veal stew suggests a fullish white on the order of a California Chardonnay or Johannisberg Riesling, or a fine, dryish Riesling from Alsace.

Bleu de Bresse While this bluish-greenish veined cheese is too assertive for a great wine, it will not necessarily overpower a robust, good wine, such as a medium-quality Hermitage, Côte Rôtie, or Châteauneuf-du-Pape. *Also see* Cheese.

Blintzes/Blinis Select a not too expensive sparkling wine, with its color and degree of sweetness dependent upon the blintzes' filling.

Blueberries As a macerating medium or as a beverage accompaniment, your best bet is a blueberry liqueur that one occasionally finds on the market. For wine selections, *see* Berries, though remember that blueberries pair less successfully with wines than do raspberries and strawberries.

Blue Cheese This family of distinctly assertive, greenish bluish-veined cheeses will distort the subtle qualities of a great wine. You are better off sticking to a robust, yet good wine like a fair quality-level Hermitage, Côte Rôtie or Châteauneuf-du-Pape. *Also see* Cheese.

Borek A coarse, inexpensive red such as a Valdepeñas (if dry) fills the bill for this Middle Eastern meat, cheese, and/or vegetable-stuffed pastry. Also consider a lager beer or ale.

Borscht Soup Since wines and soups generally don't enhance each other and since beets are not the greatest friend of wines, I recommend no wine accompaniment.

Boston Baked Beans A lager beer, ale, or hard cider stands up better than wine to this New England Indian dish.

Bouillabaisse *See* Fish.

Boursault A fullish, inexpensive red California jug wine such as the generic Burgundies is a suitable choice with this rich, creamy French cheese. *Also see* Cheese.

Boursin This herb- and garlic-laden French triple-créme cheese will overpower most wines. An inexpensive red California jug wine with some body such as a generic Burgundy is a sensible choice. *Also see* Cheese.

Braciola   Since the stuffing and even the type of rolled meat differ from recipe to recipe, it's difficult to pinpoint a precise complementary wine. In most instances, however, a Spanish Valdepeñas or an ordinary Italian Barbera is a workable red wine solution.

Brains   If prepared with a cream sauce, choose a fine white Burgundy, Graves, or California Chardonnay. If prepared with a brown sauce, serve a delicate Beaujolais of good credentials. If sautéed *beurre-noir*-style, open up a top-grade white Hermitage or perhaps a red Loire Chinon.

Bread   This staple of life is usually quite neutral and is intended to serve as a starch for the meal. Your wine choice will be determined by the other preparations served during the meal.

Brick Cheese   A quality lager beer, ale, or hard cider is a better beverage choice than a wine for this flavorful cheese. *Also see* Cheese.

Brie   A great, *Grand Cru Classé* Côte de Nuits Burgundy is the first choice for this queen of cheeses from France. Other suitable rich, full-bodied reds include the finer examples of the California Sauvignons and the top-ranked Saint-Emilions and Pomerols. *Also see* Cheese.

Bryndza   This Romanian ewe-milk cheese is much too salty for a wine, even a Romanian or Balkan one. Choose instead a lager beer or ale. *Also see* Cheese.

Butterfly/Fantail Shrimp   You need a robust, everyday white wine with sufficient body. Macon Blanc or an ordinary

California Chenin Blanc performs that role. Beer also makes a good choice, especially when the shrimp are deep-fried with a not so delicate batter. *Also see* Shellfish.

Cabbage This vegetable, even when made into properly prepared stuffed cabbage rolls, is too assertive and acidic for a fine wine. An Alsatian Gewürtztraminer is your best all-around wine choice. Lager beer or ale makes sense too.

Cacciocavallo Average-quality-level Chianti, Barbaresco, Barolo, Gattinara, and other similar medium- to full-bodied reds—including an American Zinfandel from a good producer—relate well to this flavorful Italian cheese. *Also see* Cheese.

Caerphilly An English ale, lager beer, or even stout beer seems more appropriate than a wine for this British cheese. *Also see* Cheese.

Caesar Salad The anchovies, not to mention the acidic dressing, should discourage one from serving a table wine with this famous Southwest specialty. An adequate choice is a dry fortified wine, such as a sherry or a vermouth.

Cakes (in general) Providing that the cake doesn't contain too much of one of the enemies of wine, the best all-around match-up is a Champagne or other sparkling white wine. The beverage's degree of sweetness and quality should coincide with those attributes in the cake.

Calzone Either a coarse, inexpensive red or a lager beer or ale is suitable for this puffy, hand-held Italian bread specialty that is usually stuffed with ricotta cheese and bits of ham.

Camembert With this world-famous, surface-ripened French cheese, try a parish-level Côte de Nuits Burgundy (such as Nuits-Saint-Georges or Gevrey-Chambertin), Saint-Emilion, Pomerol, Hermitage, Côte Rôtie, Châteauneuf-du-Pape, California Pinot Noir, and similar full-bodied reds. *Also see* Cheese.

Cannelloni For a discussion of pasta in general, *see* Pasta.

Caprice des Deux This rich, creamy French cheese can be sensibly companioned with a fullish, inexpensive red California jug wine such as a generic Burgundy. *Also see* Cheese.

Carbonnades Flamandes Beer is the obvious choice since this splendid beef stew is made with beer.

Carpet Bag Steak This oyster-stuffed steak, an Australian specialty, calls for a not too heavy red, such as a Valpolicella or Bardolino. An Australian Cabernet Sauvignon (which tends not to be too full) or a California Gamay may also suffice.

Carré de l'Est A Côte de Nuits Burgundy, such as a Gevrey-Chambertin or Nuits-Saint-Georges of parish-level ranking, or a Saint-Emilion, Pomerol, Hermitage, Côte Rôtie, Châteauneuf-du-Pape, California Pinot Noir, or similar full-bodied red goes well with this creamy French cheese. *Also see* Cheese.

Cassata Since this Sicilian dessert is, for the most part, lavishly covered with chocolate, a natural wine enemy, dismiss the thought of serving a wine. Instead, serve a chocolate-based liqueur, such as Vandermint, Swiss Marmot, Sabra, or Cheri-Suisse.

Cassoulet   The obvious regional choice is a red Languedoc, but such other wines as a Corbières, Chinon, or Côtes-du-Rhône-Villages make splendid substitutes, as does a California Petit Sirah or medium-grade Zinfandel.

Caviar   *See* Roe.

Ceviche   With so much acidity, this marinated South American raw fish specialty is best matched with a dry aperitif like a vermouth. If the day is hot and humid, switch to a cold beer.

Champignons à la Grecque   The substantial vinaigrette marinade dismisses table and sparkling wines from consideration. Select a dry fortified wine such as a sherry or a vermouth.

Chateaubriand   Being the most delicately textured and flavored of steaks, this expensive cut of beef cut from the center of the tenderloin deserves (if cooked medium rare) a fine red Côte de Nuits Burgundy on the order of a *Premier* or *Grand Cru* from villages such as Chamolle-Musigny, Morey-Saint-Denis, and Vosne-Romanée.

Cheddar, American   Lager beer, ale, or hard cider is your best bet. If you desire a wine, serve an inexpensive California generic Burgundy. *Also see* Cheese.

Cheddar, English   English cheeses of this sort are generally better partnered with lager beer, ale, or hard cider than with wines. Exceptions to this rule include the vintage Portos. *Also see* Cheese.

Cheese   Wine and cheese, if properly selected, are natural companions—each can bring out the best in the other. The wine trade has known of this mutually enhancing relationship for centuries, as is proven by one of their longstanding maxims: "Buy on apples, sell on cheese." Translated into layman's terms, this sagacious saying means that a tradesman should take a bite of apple before purchasing a wine because that fruit has a tendency to magnify any defects the wine may have. After having bought the wine from the vineyard, the negotiant, importer, wholesaler, or tradesperson should offer a bite of cheese to his customers because that dairy product has a penchant for glorifying the assets of wine.

The famous wine-cheese synergy is more than a personal preference; it is also a matter of science: The acid in the wine and the alkali in the cheese chemically counterbalance each other. The wine and cheese combination also offers a pleasant contrast in texture, color, aroma, and flavor.

Don't get me wrong, however; all cheeses should not automatically be paired with wine. Other beverages— especially beer and ale—can be a better foil for certain well-matured and/or strongly smelling cheeses, such as Limburger or even a powerful German Muenster. Beer and ale also go best with very salty cheeses.

Serving a cheese board at the dinner table is a rewarding experience. For a well-balanced and interesting variety consider serving one soft, one semifirm or hard, one blue vein, and one fatty goat cheese, as represented by this selection: Brie, Gruyère, Roquefort, and Valençay. Since all four are well-known cheeses, you may want to introduce one relatively unknown cheese each time you serve a cheese board. Who knows, you may fall in love with your new discovery. Whatever you select, stay away from the processed cheeses, those mass-produced commercial cheeses that do little for a wine.

Virtually all cheeses, of course, should be served at room temperature if you want to appreciate their full flavor and aroma.

My choice for the accompanying bread is a fresh and

crusty French loaf or water (wafer) biscuits. While other breads, such as rye, pumpernickel, sourdough, and Scandinavian crispbreads, are popular cheese companions, and good in their own right, I think their stronger flavor and/or texture stands in the way of enjoying the star attractions, the wine and cheese. For approximately the same reason, I don't think butter should be smeared on the accompanying bread, but don't let me stop you if you enjoy that custom.

The basic rules of matching cheese and wine are many, but the principal one for you to remember is that whenever you are in doubt, select a wine with approximately the same aroma and flavor characteristics as the cheese. Thus, serve a robust wine with a full-flavored cheese, an aromatic wine with a scented cheese, a mature wine with a well-aged cheese, a full-bodied wine with a high-fat-content cheese, a fine wine with a delicate cheese, and so on.

Like a wine, the characteristics of a cheese can vary from one end of the spectrum to the other. The cheese can be, for instance, too young or too old or at its peak of perfection—so take this variable into account.

You will find within this encyclopedia a number of individual entries for specific cheeses and cheese-based dishes. For a discussion on when to serve the cheese during a meal, *see* the subsection on formal dinners on page 29.

Cheesecake   A moderately priced sparkling red wine marries well with this rich, creamy dessert. If the Italian version (ricotta rather than cream cheese) is being served, choose a sweet Asti Spumante.

Chef's Salad   A not too sweet, commonplace rosé is the best compromise choice for this salad of hard-boiled eggs, croutons, and julienne slices of ham, turkey, tongue, and Swiss-type cheese tossed in a vinaigrette dressing.

Cherries   A better beverage accompaniment than wine for this fruit is a cherry brandy or liqueur. Kirschwasser, a brandy, is my first choice, a Peter (Cherry) Heering liqueur is a suitable alternative. Your choice of wines includes sweet French Sauternes, sweet Champagne, and sweet fortified Portos, Madeiras, Marsalas, and sherries.

Cherries Jubilee   The Cognac flambée is too much for a wine. Your best alcoholic accompaniment is the cherry brandy Kirschwasser or, as an alternative, perhaps Peter (Cherry) Heering, the Danish liqueur.

Cheshire   You are usually better off matching this English cheese with lager beer, ale, or hard cider than with wine. Exceptions to this rule include the vintage Portos. *Also see* Cheese.

Chèvre   *See* Goat Cheese.

Chicken   In terms of wine selection, you should consider chicken as possessing a neutral flavor. The wine you choose will be largely a function of the factors discussed on pages 8 to 15 (cooking method, seasoning, marinade, stuffing, garnish, and sauce) as well as freshness, age, diet, and rearing (the supermarket variety tastes blander than those raised privately or on small farms).

Although most people automatically think of white wine to go with chicken, a red often is an equal alternative and sometimes even a superior one. Generally speaking, select the white wine when the chicken is simply sautéed, poached, and/or served with a white sauce. A red is best when the chicken is roasted, barbecued, or prepared with a robust seasoning or sauce, as is the usual custom in the Mediterranean regions. Lager beer or ale more often than not also partners well with those dishes calling for a red wine. A dryish rose or dryish sparkling white wine will usually go with almost any chicken dish so long as it is not excessively seasoned.

If the wine is to be a white, it is usually medium- to full-bodied, seldom full-bodied. The proper red is light- to medium-bodied, almost never full-bodied.

For specific wine suggestions for a dozen different chicken dishes, see their individual entries in this encyclopedia.

Chicken à la King Choose a fullish white with some character, such as a California Gewürztraminer or Chenin Blanc.

Chicken Cacciatore/Chasseur The popular "hunter's chicken" harmonizes well with a somewhat robust white, such as a Macon-Villages or an Italian Orvieto. If the recipe is heavy on the tomato ingredient, switch to a robust red, such as a California Grignolino.

Chicken Fricassée A medium- to good-quality white Burgundy on the order of a village-level Chassagne- or Puligny-Montrachet. Alternatively, serve a better than average California Chardonnay.

Chicken Kiev This deep-fried, breaded chicken breast stuffed with herb butter needs a somewhat robust, yet likable, white wine, such as a Macon-Villages, a medium-grade white Hermitage, or a medium-grade California Chardonnay.

Chicken Marengo This dish was created by Napoleon's chef to help the emperor celebrate his victorious battle at Marengo, in northern Italy. The chef used whatever ingredients were available; exactly what those ingredients were is a subject of hot academic debate among food writers, but a likely list may include chicken, crayfish, onions and garlic, olive oil, tomatoes, and eggs for frying. For a wine to hold its own to this well-seasoned, hodgepodge preparation, try a robust red such as a French Corbières or a California Barbeta. A lager beer or ale also works.

Chicken Paprika   One of the best wines to stand up to this Hungarian dish is the obvious national match-up: Egri Bikaver (Bull's Blood). Domestically, try a Ruby-Cabernet. A lager beer or ale is another path to follow.

Chicken Pot Pie   Most preparations that go under this name usually deserve no better than an inexpensive California jug white, perhaps even the generic Chablis. However, if the dish is well prepared—as it can be—you can justify opening a good California Johannisberg Riesling.

Chicken Salad   An inexpensive California jug white such as the generic Chablis or a dryish rosé is more than adequate.

Chicken Soup   *See* Soup.

Chicken Tandoori   This northern Indian specialty is too assertive for a wine—drink a lager beer or ale instead.

Chicken Tetrazzini   The creamy sauce calls for a fullish white with some assertiveness, such as a California Chardonnay or a medium-grade Johannisberg Riesling.

Chicken/Turkey Mole Poblano   The chocolate plus the spices in this classic Mexican dish argue strongly against serving a wine. A lager beer or ale is a better choice.

Chiles Relleno Serve a lager beer or ale—forget about wines. The dish is simply too hot and spicy.

Chili con Carne Stick with lager beer or ale, as any wine will be overwhelmed by this well-seasoned, Texas-invented "Mexican" preparation.

Chinese Cuisine I frequently read articles and hear amateur epicures of the Western world attempting to delineate which wines make the ideal accompaniment to Chinese cuisine. Personally, speaking as an experienced Chinese cook and diner, I think their efforts are an exercise in futility. They should be addressing themselves to "whether" rather than "which" wines marry well with Chinese food. And the answer to the "whether" question is a resounding no for a variety of reasons. To begin with, most Chinese recipes, whether they come from Canton, Fukien, Shanghai, Peking, Honan, Hunan, or Szechuan, call for a significant dose of one or more ingredients (soy sauce, sugar, ginger, fermented black beans, scallions, rice vinegar, assertive spices, to name just a few) that simply debilitate whatever virtues a wine may possess. Another negative is that an authentic Chinese meal with its customary multidish offerings usually features such an assortment of flavorings that one of them is bound to argue with any wine you happen to select. A Chinese rice "wine," such as *Shaohsing*; a dry fortified wine, such as a sherry; or a lager beer or ale make better partners. If a Western world wine is really desired, a Gewürtztraminer and a modestly priced dry sparkling wine are generally the best of the inadequate alternatives— provided, of course, that your palate isn't confronted with too much sweetness, sourness, spiciness, and so forth. As for those wines such as Wan Fu that are sold in American restaurants and liquor stores, allow me to point out that they are not Chinese wines—they are French wines with Chinese characters profusely printed on their labels to give the diner the impression that he is drinking the proper wine for the ethnic food.

Chitterlings If authentically prepared, soul-food-style, serve a lager beer or ale.

Chocolate Cake Since excessive chocolate is an anathema to any wine, serve a chocolate-based liqueur, such as a Cheri-Suisse, Swiss Marmot, Sabra, or Vandermint.

Chocolate Mousse While the chocolate content of the world-famous French dessert will annihilate a wine, it is compatible with a chocolate-based liqueur, including Vandermint, Sabra, Cheri-Suisse, and Swiss Marmot.

Cholent This slow-cooked Jewish Sabbath dish calls for a robust, not too expensive red, white, or rosé, depending upon the ingredients.

Chopped Chicken Livers A modest sparkling wine is an adequate choice, though I think a lager beer or ale would partner better with this Jewish and Eastern European specialty.

Choucroute Garnie The classic affinity is a good Alsatian Gewürztraminer or a lager beer. A domestic white wine alternative is the California Gewürztraminer, but it won't be nearly as good as the French product.

Chow Mein Rather than a table wine, serve lager beer or ale—or *Shaohsing,* the Chinese rice "wine."

Christmas/Plum Pudding This classic English dessert is too rum and/or cognac infused to do any wine any good except, perhaps, a sweet fortified wine such as a Marsala.

Cioppino *See* Fish.

Clam Chowder (Manhattan and New England) *See* Soup.

Clams Casino Because of this preparation's assertive seasoning, stick to a dry, inexpensive white, or dry vermouth or sherry, or a lager beer or ale. *Also see* Shellfish.

Clams Oregano This creation is usually too seasoned for any wine except a dry sherry or vermouth, or a lager beer or ale. If your preparation is less than fully seasoned, you may opt for a dry California Sauvignon Blanc. *Also see* Shellfish.

Cod Cakes Though a lager beer or ale is preferred, you might want to try an inexpensive wine, such as a California generic Chablis.

Coeur à la Crème A fine demi-sec or doux Champagne will help cut through the rich cream and egg contents of this classic dessert. Or you may choose a sweet fortified wine of good credentials.

Cold Cuts Serve almost any red, white, or rosé wine you happen to have on hand so long as it is dryish, robust, inexpensive, slightly chilled, and drinkable.

Consommé *See* Soup.

Coq au Vin Contrary to popular notion, this dish can be made with wines other than a red Burgundy, as is the case in

Alsace, where Riesling, a white wine, is used in the recipe. Why not also try, for example, a Côtes-du-Rhône or California Gamay? Traditionally, you should drink the identical wine that went into the pan, but a substitute is indeed allowable if reasonably similar in character. The most classic of the Coq au Vins calls for the use of a Chambertin, but I personally think that while it is desirable to use a parish-level and perhaps a *Premier Cru* Gevrey-Chambertin, I wouldn't suggest wasting the *Grand Cru* Chambertin, especially if it comes from a good shipper.

Coquille Saint-Jacques If the food has been seasoned with a delicate hand, serve a wine like a white Hermitage or a good California Chardonnay. If not, serve any dryish jug white, so long as it has sufficient body. *Also see* Shellfish.

Corned Beef and Cabbage Your first choice should be a lager beer or ale, but a wine like an ordinary Beaujolais would not be wrong.

Corned Beef Hash This leftovers-inspired dish is generally too oily for a wine. Lager beer or ale makes a better alternative.

Cornish Game Hen *See* Chicken, as the guidelines are basically the same.

Coulommiers A parish-level Côte de Nuits Burgundy (such as Nuits-Saint-Georges or Gevrey-Chambertin), Saint-Emilion, Pomerol, Hermitage, Côte Rôtie, or Châteauneuf-du-Pape. California Pinot Noir, and similar full-bodied reds nicely accompany this surface-ripened French cheese. *Also see* Cheese.

Couscous A lager beer or ale or perhaps a coarse, inexpensive white or red wine (depending on the dish's main ingredients) is appropriate.

Crab Louie A modest California Chardonnay or Chenin Blanc makes a pleasant companion for this Pacific Coast specialty. *Also see* Shellfish.

Cranberry This tart Cape Cod berry doesn't get along with wines, even during a Thanksgiving dinner. There is a cranberry liqueur, but since one seldom if ever eats cranberry relish by itself, that affinity is academic.

Cream Cheese, American This popular cheese is not really an outstanding wine companion, but if one is to be served, select a lively, fresh, and fruity wine like a young Beaujolais or Loire Chinon. *Also see* Cheese.

Cream Soup *See* Soup.

Crèma Dania With this rich, creamy Danish cheese, try a fullish, inexpensive red California jug wine such as a generic Burgundy. *Also see* Cheese.

Crème Brûlée You need a quality demi-sec or doux Champagne to foil this dessert's rich egg and cream composition. A sweet fortified wine such as sherry or Madeira is another possible choice.

Crêpes (entrée) The filling determines the wine. For seafood crêpes, for instance, the cream sauce calls for a fullish white, such as a California Chardonnay or a medium-grade Côte d'Or white.

Crêpes (Dessert) While the wine depends upon the filling and the amount of sugar incorporated into the batter, you are generally safe with a Champagne or other sparkling wine so long as its quality and degree of sweetness correspond to that of the crêpe dish. With Crêpes Suzettes, the most famous of the countless crêpe specialties, the obvious and best choice is the same orange-based liqueur (Grand Marnier, Cointreau, curaçao, or Triple Sec) used in the recipe. Sweet, assertive, and fruity sparkling wines like certain Asti Spumantes are an alternative choice.

Crown Roast If the pork version, serve a brut Champagne or, perhaps, a Beaujolais-Villages. If the lamb version, serve a fine Médoc of high *Cru* status up to and including the *Premier Grand Crus*. Whether it's a pork or lamb crown roast, choose a center stuffing that is compatible with a fine wine.

Danbo A fair- to good-quality Hermitage, Côte Rôtie, Châteauneuf-du-Pape, Chianti, Rioja, Zinfandel, or other similar assertive, somewhat fruity medium- or full-bodied red pairs well with this cheese. Nonwine alternatives: a quality lager beer, ale, or hard cider. *Also see* Cheese.

Derby This English cheese is better partnered with lager beer, ale, or hard cider than with wines. Exceptions to this rule include the vintage Portos. *Also see* Cheese.

Desserts (in general) Except for certain special occasions, such as an anniversary or formal dinner, it is not a part of our modern life-style to serve a dessert wine with dessert, as this combination creates too rich and heavy a finale to an everyday repast. If you enjoy dessert wines (as I do), consider serving each guest a single two- or three-ounce portion as a now and then alternative to the dessert per se. If you desire a dessert to accompany your dessert wine during one of your everyday meals, stay clear of rich preparations and stick to peaches, nectarines, apricots, pears, and other compatible, relatively low-acidic fruits.

Even on special occasions when sweet wines and desserts are served together, you have to watch out for these all too typical desserts that are laden with sugar, lavishly laced with lemon juice or peel, overrun with chocolate, and/or embalmed with spirits, all conditions being detrimental to fine wines. When your desserts fall into any of these categories, select a suitable liqueur or sweet fortified wine, or serve a robust, medium-grade sweet sparkling wine such as the Loire Vouvray, if of an effervescent vintage. Should the dessert be macerated or soaked in a liqueur, consider serving the same liqueur. Whatever you do, save the more elegant dessert wines, such as a fine French Sauternes or a German Beerenauslese, for delicate offerings such as stone fruits and the superior members of the custard family.

For alcoholic beverage recommendations for specific desserts, refer to the appropriate entries (dozens of the more popular desserts are individually listed in this encyclopedia).

Donburi   The topping (whose variety is virtually limitless) of this Japanese rice dish determines the wine, if any.

Duck and Goose, Domesticated   Both these dark-meated, farm-raised waterbirds are well flavored and on the fatty side. Consequently, they require a big, fruity, acidic, and/or assertive wine to help counteract the high fat content. Between the two birds, the goose is the fattier and therefore needs a slightly higher degree of these wine characteristics than does the duck. While the wine selection will be greatly influenced by those factors discussed on pages 8 to 15 (cooking method, seasoning, marinade, stuffing, garnish, and sauce) as well as by the age and condition of the bird, we can generally serve with a plainly roasted duck or goose one of these wines: a better than average Médoc or Côte d'Or Burgundy; Saint-Emilions or Pomerols of reasonably fair pedigree; a good Rhône, such as a Hermitage, Côte Rôtie, or Châteauneuf-du-Pape; a Rioja of good reputation; a good California Cabernet Sauvignon or Zinfandel; or an above-average Italian Barbera, Gattinara, Barbaresco, or Chianti Classico. If a slightly lighter red is desired, try a better Beaujolais with the relative fullness of a Morgon or a Moulin-à-Vent, or a Hungarian Egri Bikaver (Bull's Blood). A brut or sec Champagne is another good choice, as is one of the big, assertive whites, particularly the Hermitage. Some Germans also prefer drinking their fine Spätlese or even Auslese Rieslings of the Rhine with duck and goose.

Often duck is prepared Bigarade-style (with orange sauce) or Montmorency-style (with cherry sauce). Both these preparations are too sweet and sour for a fine wine. An acceptable compromise would be a sec Champagne of humble origin.

Pressed duck prepared the French way calls for a good Burgundy or Bordeaux, while one prepared in the Chinese manner cannot be suitably matched with wine.

Goose is popularly stuffed with apples, prunes, and/or a well-seasoned sausage—ingredients that can stand in your way in the appreciation of a fine wine. Should you decide to go ahead and cook your own goose in this manner, select no better than an average-grade sec Champagne or, perhaps, an ordinary Gewürztraminer.

Duckling à l'Orange   *See* Duck and Goose, Domesticated.

Dunlop A better choice than wine for this English cheese is usually a lager beer, ale, or hard cider. Exceptions to this rule include the vintage Portos. *Also see* Cheese.

Éclair *See* Pastries.

Edam A quality lager beer or ale pairs best with this Dutch cheese. If a wine is desired, select a somewhat coarse and fullish one, such as a California generic Burgundy or a Petit Sirah. *Also see* Cheese.

Egg Egg yolks and wine are not compatible, as the former, under the proper circumstances, can give wine an un-pleasant off-flavor, the result of a chemical reaction. This is not to say that the slight use of an egg yolk in a sauce will do considerable harm to a fine wine (though an egg-yolk-rich sauce, such as a Hollandaise, certainly would). Neither will a straight egg dish, such as a plain omelet or poached eggs, play damnation upon a properly selected everyday wine (though it would upon a wine possessing delicate nuances). For a fuller discussion of eggs, *see* relevant individual entries: Omelet, etc. For background information on egg-based desserts, *see* Desserts.

Egg Foo Yung Serving a table wine with this Chinese dish doesn't make sense because of both its egg yolk content and the cooking method required by it. A Chinese rice wine is probably your best bet should you want an alcoholic beverage accompaniment.

Eggplant Parmigiana Choose a robust, acidy, inexpen-sive red much on the order of the typical Sicilian Etna wines that are imported into this country. Any red California generic Burgundy, if not too sweet, is also suitable for this tomatoey and assertively seasoned Neapolitan specialty.

Egg Rolls   Enjoy this Chinese specialty with lager beer or ale or the Chinese *Shaohsing* rice "wine."

Eggs à la Russe   Forgo table wines because of this appetizer's heavy egg yolk and spice content. Better choices are a dry fortified wine such as a sherry, a white vermouth of good quality, or a Madeira.

Eggs Benedict   Tradition calls for a sparkling white, and I suppose this is as good as any because of the heavy fat content incorporated in three of the dish's principal ingredients: egg yolks, butter, and ham. An alternative is an ordinary, fullish, assertive white, such as a medium-grade Sancerre, or a light-bodied, fresh, young red on the order of an unassuming Beaujolais. Whatever you serve, because of the excessive amount of egg yolks that are found both in the poached eggs per se and in the Hollandaise sauce, don't spend too much.

Eggs Florentine   This dish, because of its abundance of egg yolks and spinach, is really not on friendly terms with wine. If one is to be served, out of deference to all the principal ingredients, including the Mornay-type sauce, pour an ordinary, assertive white with some body. A California-produced French Colombard or a modestly priced sparkling white fulfills this mission.

Emmenthaler   While the best national match-up for this cheese is the red Swiss Dole, you are usually better off with a fair- to good-quality Hermitage, Côte Rôtie, Châteauneuf-du-Pape, Chianti, Rioja, Zinfandel, or other similar assertive, somewhat fruity medium- or full-bodied red. Nonwine alternatives: a quality lager beer, ale, or hard cider. *Also see* Cheese.

Enchiladas In almost every case a lager beer or ale is the wisest choice.

English Mixed Grill A good British beer or ale is the prime choice for this hearty meat combo dish. If you do serve a wine, stick with a modest, robust red, such as a young Zinfandel or modest Rioja.

Esrom A Côte de Beaune (village-level), Morgon or Moulin-à-Vent Beaujolais, California Zinfandel, Mercurey, Rully, or other similar medium-bodied red combines successfully with this Danish cheese. *Also see* Cheese.

Feta This Greek ewe-milk cheese is much too salty for a wine, even a Greek one. Choose instead a lager beer or ale. *Also see* Cheese.

Fettucini Alfredo *See* Pasta.

Filet Mignon If simply grilled or roasted, serve a fine red Côte d'Or Burgundy; Bonnes Mares and Musigny are two good choices, as is a *Premier* or *Grand Cru* from Vosne-Romanée. One of the better examples of the California Pinot Noir works well too.

Finnan Haddie Select a lager beer or ale for this Scottish smoked-fish specialty.

Fish If you want a simple guideline for selecting a wine to accompany a fish dish, you probably won't go too wrong by choosing a crisp or relatively crisp, dry or bone-dry, medium- or full-bodied, still or sparkling white wine with at least some acidity. Many, many wines more or less satisfy these criteria. For your quick-reference convenience, here is but a brief sampling of the popular white wine choices: Chablis, Champagne, Chardonnay, Chenin Blanc, Côte d'Or (up to and including the *Premier* and *Grand Cru* wines), Graves, Hermitage, Johannisberg Riesling, Macon Blanc, Macon-Villages, Muscadet, Orvieto, Pouilly-Fuissé, Pouilly-Fumé, Rioja, Riesling (dry), Sancerre, Soave, Verdicchio, and Vinho Verde.

However, for the more serious wine-food affinity sleuth, the proper selection of a wine to match a particular fish dish is exceedingly more complex than the pat answers provided in the preceding paragraph. We must take into consideration not only the type of fish but also its freshness as well as how it was cooked, sauced, seasoned, and garnished. When you put all these variables together, you have a virtually infinite number of permutations—obviously too many to individually describe or even list in a book of this size (it would take a series of books to do the job comprehensively).

Since there are so many possibilities of different combinations among the variables (fish type, cooking method, etc.), the only logical way to approach the wine selection problem is to try to understand the parameters of each of those variables, one by one, on an isolated basis. Then, when confronted with a particular fish preparation, we can come up with a sort of "reasoned out" solution. For instance, with Sole à la Normande, the fish type suggests a medium-bodied white, but the cream sauce calls for a fuller bodied white with more character and fruit, such as a good white Côte d'Or, so we either choose the latter type of wine or cut down on the portion of sauce served with the fish, in which case we would serve a still good, but somewhat lighter wine, such as an estate-bottled Muscadet de Sèvre-et-Maine.

First, let us learn how the type of fish helps dictate our

wine choice. Generally, the fattier the fish, the fuller bodied, more assertive, and/or fruitier the white wine should be (though in certain circumstances it is possible to serve a rosé or light-bodied red, as I will explain later; for the time being we will be thinking exclusively in terms of white wines). To help you determine, at a glance, the fat content of some sixty popular varieties of fish and other seafood, I have prepared this quick-reference chart based upon official U.S. Government data:

Abalone (0.5% fat content)
Alewife (4.9%)
Anchovies, canned (10.3%)
Barracuda, Pacific (2.6%)
Black sea bass (2.3%)
Bluefish (3.3%)
Butterfish, northern waters (10.2%)
Butterfish, gulf waters (2.9%)
Caviar, sturgeon (15.0%)
Clams (0.9 to 1.9%)
Cod (0.3%)
Crab (1.9%)
Crayfish (0.5%)
Croaker, Atlantic (2.2%)
Eel (18.3%)
Frogs' legs (0.3%)
Haddock (0.1%)
Hake (0.4%)
Halibut, U.S. (1.2 to 1.4%)
Herring, Atlantic (11.3%)
Herring, Pacific (2.6%)
Herring, kippers (12.9%)
Herring, pickled (15.1%)
Lake herring (2.3%)
Lake trout (10.0%)

Lobster, Maine (1.9%)
Lobster, spiny (0.5%)
Mackerel, Atlantic (12.2%)
Mackerel, Pacific (7.3%)
Mullet (6.9%)
Mussels (2.2%)
Oysters (1.8 to 2.2%)
Pike (4.1 to 5.4%)
Pollack (0.9%)
Ocean perch, Atlantic (1.2 to 1.5%)
Octopus (0.8%)
Red snapper (0.9%)
Rockfish (1.8%)
Salmon (13.4 to 15.6%)
Salmon roe (10.4%)
Sardines, canned (11.1 to 12.2%)
Scallops, bay and sea (0.2%)
Sea bass (0.5%)
Shad (10.0%)
Shad roe (1.5%)
Sheepshead, Atlantic (5.2%)
Shrimp (0.8%)
Smelts (2.1 to 6.2%)
Snails (1.4%)
Squid (0.9%)
Striped bass (2.7%)
Sturgeon (1.9%)
Swordfish (4.0%)
Tilefish (0.5%)
Trout, brook (2.1%)
Trout, rainbow (11.4%)
Tuna (3.0 to 4.1%)
Tuna, canned (8.2%)
Terrapin (3.5%)

Turtle, green (0.5%)
Weakfish (5.6%)
Whale meat (7.5%)
White sea bass (2.3%)
Whiting (3.0%)
Yellowtail (5.4%)

We must also take into consideration how a fish tastes, a variable that covers the full spectrum, ranging from such fishes as freshly caught sole, red snapper, pompano, trout, and red mullet to the stronger flavored fishes, like herring. Save your great wines for the milder group while serving assertive, middle-quality wines (regional-level white Burgundies, Orvieto, etc.) for the second group. Lager beer and ale also pair well with the latter.

Other variables include the intrinsic difference in the quality of distinct fishes. Red snapper has a flavor superior to that of lemon sole, for instance, and demands a better quality wine. Likewise, a lemon sole is better than a gray sole and thereby deserves a better wine. Thus, while a *Premier Cru* Côte d'Or white may be just the ticket for the red snapper, the lemon sole can be happy with a Macon-Villages, and the gray sole with an ordinary white such as one of the dryish California jug whites.

Still another variable is where the fish lived. For the most part, fish that swim in cool waters have better flavor and texture than those that live in warm waters. The same differences are generally true between the fish that resides in still water, be it a lake or the ocean, and the fish that swims in a fast-moving river (the extra exercise tends to give the latter fish a superior flavor).

Even the quality of two fish of the same species can vary from one fishing bank or river to another. Perhaps the most striking example is the difference in taste and texture between a "wild" trout caught in a cold mountain brook and its "domestic" identical twin that was raised on a commercial trout farm. The latter will be significantly flabbier and less flavorful than its "born free" sibling, to the point where your educated palate falsely concludes they are entirely different fish species.

The taste of an ocean-to-river spawning fish can vary according to where it is caught. A salmon, for instance, is best when it has just started its journey up the river. The exhausting upstream trek physically takes so much out of the salmon that by the time it has spawned and begun its return to the sea, it is less of a prize for a gourmet fisherman.

The second major wine selection variable is the freshness of the fish. The longer a fish has been dead and/or the worse it has been stored, the less delicate and more fishy (a negative quality) the creature will be. Also, needless to say, the virtues of a fish that hasn't been frozen are superior to those that have met Jack Frost, and thus generally deserve a better wine.

How the fish is cooked is our third major wine selection determinant. A plainly grilled or broiled fish will not obscure the subtleties of a fine wine; neither will a panfried fish, cooked in no more than a minimum amount of fresh oil or butter. On the other end of the spectrum are deep-fried fish, and especially those coated with a coarse batter; serve an everyday, robust white—or a lager beer or ale.

Our remaining three wine selection determinants—the sauce, the seasoning, and the garnish—are especially important because fish, like chicken, is basically a neutral food. As the discussion of this topic on pages 12 to 15 suggests, save your great wines for the fish preparations that are gently seasoned and that have garnishes and savors that are compatible with wine. This restriction eliminates, for instance, Hollandaise (too much egg yolk), tartare, and those tomato-, onion-, and garlic-rich Mediterranean sauces. A Normandy-type sauce, on the other hand, is certainly fine enough to warrant a fine wine—but make sure the wine is sufficiently full-bodied to cut across the sauce's cream, egg yolk, and butter content. Specific suggestions for such sauces include the big white Côte d'Ors and Rhônes, the top-of-the-line California Chardonnays, and the quality, dry sparkling wines, including Champagne. A simply cooked fish of delicate flavor—such as a freshly caught trout—calls for a medium-bodied white like a fine German or Alsatian Riesling, if not too sweet.

Fish stews, by their very nature and purpose, are seldom delicately seasoned and therefore require a more assertive white, something like an Orvieto or dryish Provence white. A quality fish stew, such as a well-made Bouillabaisse, still needs an assertive wine, but in this case you could spend a few extra dollars and buy a good white Hermitage or better than average California Chardonnay.

Smoked salmon (lox, nova, etc.), kippers, bloaters, finnan haddie, canned tuna and sardines, salt cod, pickled herring, and other preserved fish specialties are better paired with a lager beer or ale; a dry fortified wine such as a sherry or vermouth; or a fiery white spirit, such as schnapps. If a wine is desired, a dry, medium-quality sparkling white is your best alternative.

Most wine drinkers in America automatically think in terms of serving white wine with fish. Yet, there are instances where a light-bodied red, such as a regional-level Chalonnais or Loire, or a dry rosé, is a suitable alternative to a white wine. One example is the French Matelote, a fish stew that is generally made with a light-bodied red. If you do serve a red wine, your chief precaution should be to avoid one with more than a moderate amount of tannin because an unpleasant flavor develops when the tannic acid chemically reacts with the halogens (such as iodine) that are normally found in fish.

You will find further related discussions under Roe and Shellfish.

Fish en Papillote   *See* Fish.

Flan   Select a demi-sec or doux sparkling wine, the quality being dependent on the quality of the preparation. Alternatively, opt for a sweet fortified wine such as a Porto or Madeira, but again, matching quality for quality.

Fondue, Bourguignonne   The hot cooking oil clinging to the cubed beef and the assertiveness of one or more of the accompanying sauces precludes a fine wine, but a robust red like a Côtes-du-Rhône or a California Petit Sirah is a good choice.

Fondue, Cheese   A white Neuchâtel is the traditional wine ingredient in this Swiss specialty, and therefore it is logical to serve it as the accompanying wine. But because of the fondue's significant cheese content you would not be iconoclastic if you served a light-bodied red, such as a Swiss Dole. Or, as some Swiss families do, drink tea.

Fondue, Chocolate   Stay completely away from wines because of the overpowering chocolate content. A chocolate-based liqueur, such as a Vandermint, Sabra, or Cheri-Suisse, would be more suitable for this dessert dish.

Fontina   Chianti, Barbaresco, Barolo, Gattinara, and other similar medium- to full-bodied reds—including an American Zinfandel from a fine producer—relate well with this flavorful Italian cheese. *Also see* Cheese.

Fritto-Misto   An Orvieto wine or lager beer or ale are good selections for this Italian "mixed fried" specialty.

Frogs' Legs à la Provençale   The heavy garlic flavoring dismisses a fine wine from consideration. A middle-quality white southern Burgundy, such as a Macon, or a not too fine white Rhône is a sound choice. Don't forget lager beer or ale, too.

Fruit Tarts   A luscious French Sauternes is the classic affinity with a berry or stone-fruit tart, and especially if it is garnished with whipped cream, which serves to help lessen any lingering acidity in the fruit mixture. If the tart is fresh and splendidly prepared, this is an ideal opportunity to open up a Château d'Yquem, the empress of French Sauternes. Alternatives to a Sauternes include a fine, sweet (demi-sec or doux) Champagne, a German Beerenauslese, a five-*puttonyos* Hungarian Tokay, and possibly a sweet fortified wine. A liqueur that matches the fruit would be good also.

Fruits de Mer/Frutti di Mare   *See* Fish.

Fruit Salad   If the ingredients include one or more citrus fruits (as most fruit salads do), then don't choose a wine; the same is true if the fruit salad contains banana or pineapple. Your best option in these instances is to select a suitable fruit-based liqueur (*see* individual fruit entries). A sweet dessert wine, a sweet Champagne, or a sweet fortified wine such as a Porto or Madeira goes well with fruit salads comprising peaches, nectarines, cherries, pears, and/or berries, providing that all are in their prime. The latter fruits all marry well with their liqueur or brandy counterparts.

Fruit Soup   No wine is your best course of action. *See* Soup.

Game   Wine selection will be determined principally by the kind of animal and its feeding ground, and by those factors discussed on pages 8 to 15 (aging, cooking method, seasoning, marinade, stuffing, garnish, and sauce).

For the sake of convenience, let us classify game into three categories: large four-legged game, small four-legged game, and game birds. The first category, large four-legged game, includes such beasts as deer (venison), elk, moose, and bear. Their meats (if plainly roasted) need a big full-flavored red such as a Côte de Nuits Burgundy on the order of a solid Gevrey-Chambertin or Fixin; a Rhône such as a Côte Rôtie, Hermitage, or Châteauneuf-du-Pape; a northern Italian of the pedigree of a Barolo or Chianti Classico. Generally, the older the animal and/or the longer the meat is hung, the fruitier and more assertive the wine should be—thus, a young, unhung and unmarinated venison would do well with a softer Côte d'Or such as a Pommard or Volnay from the Côte de Beaune or a not too big California Pinot Noir. Another possibility is a Rhine Spätlese or even an Auslese, as is the custom in Germany, but the use of a wine with that degree of sweetness may not suit everyone, as it is very much an acquired taste.

Our second category, small four-legged game, includes wild boar, hare, and wild rabbit. When plainly roasted, their somewhat full-flavored meats go well with the Morgons and Moulin-à-Vents of Beaujolais, as well as the better Zinfandels of California. If served in a stew, as in Hassenpfeffer, Civet de Lièvre, or Jugged Hare, you may wish to open a Côte de Beaune Burgundy such as a parish-level Pommard or Volnay, or a California Pinot Noir. For the generally more common Brunswick Stew, open a more ordinary red.

Game birds, our third category, include wild duck, wild goose, wild turkey, pheasant, partridge, quail, grouse, doves, squab, guinea fowl, and those small delectable winged creatures like ortolan, plover, snipe, lark, and woodcock. For the wild duck and goose, follow the wine selections suggested under Duck and Goose, Domesticated but opt for one of the slightly more assertive wines. Also keep in mind that some wild ducks are fish eaters and, consequently, are not exactly of tantalizing flavor. For the small game birds that are plainly roasted (a good idea), I recommend a fine big white like one of the *Premier* or *Grand Cru* Côte de Beaune whites from the villages of Chassagne-Montrachet, Puligny-Montrachet, or Meursault, or a classified red Médoc or Graves. For those in-between game birds such as the pheasant and quail you have a good opportunity for uncorking a fine Saint-Emilion or Pomerol—or a *Premier* or *Grand Cru* Côte de Beaune, perhaps a Volnay. As a general rule, go up the wine assertiveness scale as the age of the bird and the length of hanging time (if any) increases. But go down the scale whenever any of these game birds have been commercially raised, which happens more often than most people suspect.

For all three of the above categories, a brut or sec Champagne provides you with a good alternative.

Whenever you're having a fine wine, avoid serving those traditional fruit accompaniments such as currant, mint, and other jellies. The same goes for fruit garnishes. Each tends to diminish your palate's capacity for detecting the subtle nuances of a topflight wine.

For game fish, *see* Fish.

Gammelost   A quality lager beer or ale is better than a wine for this pungent Norwegian cheese. *Also see* Cheese.

Gazpacho   This cold Andalusian soup-salad is much too strongly flavored to do a wine any service. Relish it on its own terms, by itself.

Gefilte Fish   Serve an inexpensive, robust white or, even better, a lager beer or ale with this Jewish fish-ball specialty that is often accompanied by grated horseradish.

Gjetost   A lager beer or ale is a wiser choice than wine for this out-of-the-ordinary-tasting Norwegian cheese. *Also see* Cheese.

Gloucester, Double or Single   With this English cheese, you are generally wiser to serve a lager beer, ale, or hard cider than a wine. Exceptions to this rule include the vintage Portos. *Also see* Cheese.

Gnocchi   Made with potatoes and/or wheat flour, this Italian staple should be treated like pasta *(see)* when it comes to wine selection.

Goat   If plainly roasted and young (kid), open a red with some character, such as a Côtes-du-Rhône-Villages or a medium-grade Zinfandel. If the cooking instructions or whim call for strong herbs and garlic, as is customary in some parts of the Mediterranean world, serve an everyday red, such as a California generic Burgundy. If the meat is delicately prepared, try a basic Barolo, Chianti, or Gattinara.

Goat Cheese   Run-of-the-mill goat-milk cheese pairs well with young, fresh, and lively wines like Beaujolais, certain red Loires (Chinon, etc.), and the California Gamay Noir. Excellent goat-milk cheeses such as Saint-Marcellin, Montrachet, and Valençay are beautifully set with a fine red Côte de Beaune Burgundy, such as a Volnay or Pommard. *Also see* Cheese.

Goose   *See* Duck and Goose, Domesticated.

Gorgonzola   This Italian bluish-greenish veined cheese will overpower a great wine, but it will not necessarily be too assertive for a robust yet good wine such as a medium-quality Chianti, Hermitage, Côte Rôtie, or Châteauneuf-du-Pape. *Also see* Cheese.

Gouda A good companion for this Dutch cheese is a quality lager beer or ale. If a wine is desired, select a somewhat coarse and fullish one such as a California generic Burgundy or a Petit Sirah. *Also see* Cheese.

Grape Tart, lackluster table grapes like the ubiquitous Thompson seedless bring out the worst in a wine, notwithstanding the fact that both are grape items. The same is true for all grapes employed in making wine or raisins. Some of the quality table grapes, if perfectly ripe, on the other hand, can complement a medium-grade French Sauternes, a top-grade Montbazillac, or similar sweet dessert wines.

Grapefruit All citrus produce, including this one, are enemies of wine. If you wish a beverage accompaniment or a macerating medium, you may consider Forbidden Fruit, a liqueur (it is a brandy that has been infused, in part, with grapefruit).

Green Turtle Soup You probably shouldn't be serving a wine with a soup, but if you crave one, drink the same dry fortified wine that has been used in the recipe (more than likely, this will be a Madeira or sherry).

Gruyère I suggest for this cheese a fair- to good-quality Hermitage, Côte Rôtie, Châteauneuf-du-Pape, Chianti, Rioja, Zinfandel, or another similar assertive, somewhat fruity medium- or full-bodied red. Best national match-up: the red Swiss Dole. Nonwine alternatives: a quality lager beer, ale, or hard cider. *Also see* Cheese.

Guacamole Dip Lager beer or ale rather than wine goes best with this oniony, spicy avocado Mexican specialty.

Gumbo (Chicken, etc.) If the soup has been thinly made, forget about wines (*see* Soup). If it has been thickly prepared, you can serve a not too costly white wine assertive enough to stand up to the strong flavoring and tomatoes in this soup-stew. An Italian Orvieto, a Loire Gros Plant, or a California Colombard helps fulfill that goal.

Ham This cured pork joint can be matched with a light- to medium-bodied red with some acid (Burgundy, for example), a medium- to full-bodied white (Vouvray, etc.), a rosé (Tavel, Cabernet Rosé d'Anjou, among others), or a sparkling wine—as long as your selected wine is not expensive and is sufficiently assertive to stand up to the ham's high fat content as well as its significant smoke and salt flavor. Some hams, such as the Smithfield variety, are excessively salt infused, so be sure to presoak the ham long enough to leech out a great deal of its salt if you plan to drink even a medium-grade wine (otherwise, stick to an inexpensive jug-type wine).

Also watch out for those popular fruit garnishes like pineapple, as they don't do favors for wine. Neither do cloves (while a clove-studded ham is photogenic, the many cloves ruin both the wine and the ham, not to mention a tooth now and then). Should you sweet-glaze your ham, increase the desired sweetness of your wine proportionally—but do not have either the glaze or the wine too sweet lest the dish become unpleasantly cloying.

Hamburgers You have many choices, including a simple, somewhat assertive red, such as California-jug generic

Burgundy or perhaps a young, not too expensive Zinfandel or Côtes-du-Rhône. Don't overlook lager beer or ale.

Havarti Much better than wine for this flavorful Danish cheese is a lager beer, ale, or hard cider. *Also see* Cheese.

Hot and Sour Soup No wine is sufficiently bold enough to stand up to this spicy Chinese soup. Besides, a soup is best enjoyed without a liquid accompaniment, be it wine or beer.

Hot and Spicy Dishes Wine is not complemented by hot and spicy dishes, as the seasoning in the food renders your palate insensitive to whatever subtleties the wine may offer. A lager beer or ale is often a better alcoholic beverage selection. If you must serve a wine, select an inexpensive Gewürtztraminer or a modestly priced dry sparkling wine.

Hot Dogs A jug red or rosé is the highest you should go up the wine-quality scale for this all-American sausage. If it has been well garnished with mustard, onions, and/or sauerkraut, switch to a lager beer or ale.

Huevos à la Flamenca Virtually all wines are overwhelmed by this assertively flavored Spanish egg dish. Perhaps a coarse, inexpensive jug white would not be out of character, but a lager beer, ale, or hard cider would be more preferable.

Huevos Rancheros This Mexican dish is too assertive for even the coarsest, least expensive wines—but if you want to serve such an unpretentious beverage, go ahead, as the waste will be minimal. Lager beer, ale, or hard cider, however, is a sounder choice.

Hungarian Goulash One of the best match-ups for this zesty stew is the Egri Bikaver (Bull's Blood) of Hungary. A domestic alternative is the California Petit Sirah.

Ice Cream The rich cream, egg yolk, and sugar content, not to mention the other flavoring ingredients in ice cream, argue against serving a wine. Your wisest choice is a liqueur, ideally one whose flavor matches up with the ice cream.

Ices/Sherbets Ices and sherbets are best enjoyed by themselves. A suitable liqueur may suffice in certain situations, but don't count on it.

Indian Cuisine *See* Hot and Spicy Dishes. However, bear in mind that northern Indian cooking is not as strongly seasoned as the southern variety and is thereby better suited for a wine if the wine is robust and you don't spend too much for it.

Indian Pudding The strong molasses flavor precludes any wine or liqueur.

Irish Stew If the dish has been well made, a Beaujolais-Villages or medium-grade Zinfandel is in order. Otherwise, stick to lager beer or ale, the best all-around choice.

Jambalaya Depending on the ingredients, this Creole specialty can be partnered with a somewhat fullish white or a dryish rosé. Either way, the wine should be reasonably assertive and inexpensive. Filling these criteria are the French district-level white Macons and the California Gewürztraminers (if not too sweet), Grignolinos, and Grenache Rosés. A sound alternative to wine is lager beer or ale.

Jarlsberg   Uncork a fair- to good-quality Hermitage, Côte Rôtie, Châteauneuf-du-Pape, Chianti, Rioja, Zinfandel, or other similar assertive, somewhat fruity medium- or full-bodied red with this Norwegien cheese. Nonwine alternatives: a quality lager beer, ale, or hard cider. *Also see* Cheese.

Kasha Varnitchkes   The assertive flavor of buckwheat in this Jewish groats and bowtie-shaped-noodle dish is far better matched with beer than with any wine, save the not too sweet jug whites.

Kidneys, Veal   If the kidneys have been plainly grilled, a good Saint-Emilion or Pomerol is an excellent choice. If they have been well seasoned, as in a casserole dish, switch to a lesser Saint-Emilion or Pomerol. Generally, the older the calf from which the kidneys were obtained, the lesser the quality of wine you should buy.

Kippers   An English beer or ale—or a schnappslike liquor—suits this cured fish.

Kishke   An Alsatian Gewürtztraminer, a lager beer, or an ale are good choices for this Jewish specialty.

Kobe Steak   Should you be fortunate enough to come across this exceedingly tender cut of steak from Japan, open up a superb Côte de Nuits Burgundy; Clos de Vougeot and Grands Échézeaux are two splendid options.

Kulebiaka   When expertly made, this superb Russian specialty deserves a *Premier* or *Grand Cru* white Burgundy—up to and including Le Montrachet. One of California's best Chardonnays would not be out of order either.

Lamb The classic affinity for lamb is a red Bordeaux wine because, among other valid reasons, the wine's tannin helps cut through the normal fattiness of the meat. But the "serve Bordeaux with lamb" rule is too much of an oversimplification to do much good. There are just too many different types of Bordeaux wine. Moreover, the characteristics of the meat vary significantly as a function of its age.

The meat is (or should be) classified as baby lamb if under three months old, as regular lamb if between three and twelve months old, and as mutton once it reaches its first birthday. Baby lamb is the tenderest and most delicate-flavored of all, while mutton is the least tender and is rather full-flavored. With the baby lamb (if it has been simply roasted or grilled with minimal seasonings), you can open up your finest old Medoc, including that 1955 Château Lafite-Rothschild. With mutton, however, I wouldn't support anything better than a somewhat coarse but good red with enough body, fruit, and acidity to stand up to the meat's fattiness and strong flavor—a wine like one of the lower-priced California Cabernet Sauvignons does the trick.

For the in-between stage—lamb between three and twelve months of age—you have a fair range of wines with sufficient body, fruit, assertiveness, and acidity to counteract the meat's fattiness and pronounced flavor, examples being the better versions of some of these wines: California Cabernet Sauvignons and Zinfandels, the Italian Barolos and Chiantis, the Spanish Riojas, and of course, the various Médoc châteaux of celebrated but not noble stature.

Other acceptable choices, if you want a lighter red, are a Beaujolais of at least *Village* ranking; the better red Loires, such as Chinon; the top-grade Valpolicellas; and the above-average Corbières and Dãos.

Should you well-season your lamb with strong herbs and perhaps garlic, as is the popular custom in the Mediterranean lands, switch to a tougher wine, such as a medium-grade

Hermitage, Châteauneuf-du-Pape, or Chianti, letting the quality of the wine be determined by the cut of meat and the degree of seasoning. Between the two most popular cuts of lamb, the chops are fattier than the meat cut from the leg, so bear this in mind in your wine selection process. Other factors to heed include the cooking method, the sauce, and the seasoning (*see* pages 8 to 15).

Lamb Navarin　A Médoc on the order of a medium- to top-level Saint-Estèphe is a good choice for this sophisticated stew. A California Cabernet Sauvignon on the same quality level is a worthy domestic wine choice. If mutton is used instead of lamb (as in Navarin de Mouton), go down the wine-quality scale.

Lamb Villeroi　A mature, top-grade Spanish Rioja (or a California Zinfandel with equal credentials) will stand up to these lamb chops coated first with a reduced and enriched Allemande sauce, second with beaten egg, and third with bread crumbs prior to being sautéed in butter. Out of deference to the wine, select youngish lamb—and try keeping down to a minimum the eggs you use in both the Allemande sauce and the beaten egg coating.

Lancashire　Rather than thinking in terms of wine, opt for a lager beer, ale, or hard cider for this English cheese. Exceptions to this rule include the vintage Portos. *Also see* Cheese.

Lasagna　*See* Pasta.

Leicester　This breed of English cheeses has a better match with lager beer, ale, or hard cider than with wines. Exceptions to this rule include the vintage Portos. *Also see* Cheese.

Lemon This astringent citrus fruit is one of wine's greatest enemies, especially when used in more than minute proportions as a flavoring agent in a culinary preparation.

Lemon Chicken There is simply too much acidity in this dish to suit a wine, even the more modest ones. A Chinese rice "wine," such as *Shaohsing*, or lager beer or ale is the better course to follow.

Leyden A quality lager beer, ale, or hard cider is a better beverage choice than a wine for this cumin-and-caraway-flavored Dutch cheese. *Also see* Cheese.

Liederkranz A strong beer, not a wine, is demanded by this assertive, odoriferous American cheese. *Also see* Cheese.

Limburger Select a full-flavored beer instead of a wine for this strong-smelling German and Belgian cheese. *Also see* Cheese.

Lime Beware of using this flavoring agent in more than minute amounts if you are serving a wine—and especially if your wine is a fine one.

Liver, Calf's If the liver has been gently sautéed in butter with a touch of onions, as is the style of Lyons, Switzerland, and Venice, serve a medium- to good-grade Médoc or California Cabernet Sauvignon, or those two relatively big Beaujolais, Moulin-à-Vent and Morgon. On the white wine side, serve a top-grade California Johannisberg Riesling. Should the liver be more assertively prepared and seasoned, choose a correspondingly more robust wine, perhaps an average Beaujolais or Valpolicella. If the liver approaches or becomes beef rather than calf's liver, switch to a modest jug red, such as the California generic Burgundy.

Lobster à l'Américaine   Serve the same wine used to make the dish—or perhaps open a light, acidy red Loire, such as a Chinon. *Also see* Shellfish.

Lobster Bisque   *See* Soup.

Lobster Cantonese   A lager beer or ale, a Chinese rice "wine," or a dry fortified wine such as sherry is your best bet. *Also see* Shellfish.

Lobster Cardinale   A fine Côte d'Or white Burgundy, perhaps of *Premier Cru* status, makes a fine choice for this rich, creamy dish. *Also see* Shellfish.

Lobster Fra Diavolo   This dish is too spicy for anything but a lager beer or ale. *Also see* Shellfish.

Lobster Newburg   The best wine selection is the dry fortified wine (sherry or Madeira) used in the sauce. A lager beer or ale is also a good choice. *Also see* Shellfish.

Lobster à la Parisienne   This classic French cold lobster dish calls for a white, full enough to cut through the mayonnaise, but because of the wine-hostile garnish, a fine wine would be wasted. A good solution would be a good but not great white Hermitage, Pouilly-Fumé, or Sancerre.

Lobster Thermidor   A wine such as a medium-quality California Chârdonnay or Chenin Blanc, or perhaps a good white Rioja does this dish justice, as does a lager beer, an ale, a dry vermouth, and a dry sherry or Madeira. *Also see* Shellfish.

Lo Mein   Generally, the Chinese rice "wine" *Shaohsing* or a lager beer or ale are the best accompaniments to this Chinese noodle dish.

London Broil   Serve a not too fine but acidy wine like a red Loire or a young California Zinfandel, or a modestly priced Chianti.

Macaroni and Cheese   *See* Pasta.

Manicotti   *See* Pasta.

Maryland Crab Cakes   Lager beer or ale should be your first choice, but if you crave a wine, select a dry, ordinary wine with some assertiveness and body, such as a California Colombard. *Also see* Shellfish.

Matzo Ball Soup   Some things in life are better consumed by themselves, and this includes this Jewish mainstay. *Also see* Soup.

Meat Loaf   A common California red jug wine is a suitable accompaniment.

Melon   Much superior than wines for the melon fruit family are medium-sweet Portos, Madeiras, Marsalas, and similar fortified wines.

Mexican Cuisine   *See* Hot and Spicy Dishes. However, keep in mind that a few Mexican dishes are sufficiently low-keyed to be matched with appropriate robust, inexpensive red or white wines; Gallo's Hearty Burgundy is one example.

Mille-Feuilles *See* Pastries.

Minestrone This soup is generally thick enough to warrant a dry fortified wine, but you are probably better off relishing this vegetable and pasta (or rice) Italian nourishment by itself.

Minute Steak While too common and coarse for a fine wine, a modestly priced red Rioja or Côtes-du-Rhône-Villages would satisfy your needs.

Misoshiru *See* Soup.

Moo Goo Gai Pan A Chinese rice "wine" or a lager beer or ale partner better with this Chinese chicken and mushroom dish than does a wine.

Montrachet A fine red Côte de Beaune Burgundy like a Volnay or Pommard marry well with this French goat-milk cheese. *Also see* Cheese.

Monterey Jack A top-notch California Pinot Noir (or perhaps a fair Cabernet Sauvignon or a better-grade Zinfandel) is a perfect companion for this California cheese. *Also see* Cheese.

Moules à la Marinière Serve the same wine you used to make this dish. Ideally, the wine will be something like a dry, crisp Muscadet, particularly one with Sèvre-et-Maine heritage. *Also see* Shellfish.

Moussaka The Greek Retsina or Kokkineli is excellent because the resin flavor helps cuts through the oiliness in this dish. A medium-grade California Zinfandel or lager beer or ale is another sound option.

Mozzarella   When the mozzarella is used as an eating as opposed to a cooking cheese, serve a fair-quality Chianti or, perhaps, a dryish Lambrusco. *Also see* Cheese.

Mozzarella in Carrozza   A Bardolino and, even more so, a Valpolicella complement this toasted ham and cheese "sandwich," an Italian specialty.

Muenster   A better beverage choice than wine for this flavorful cheese is a quality lager beer, ale, or hard cider. *Also see* Cheese.

Mulligatawny Soup   This British-devised Indian "pepper water" specialty is too assertive, with its curry spices, for most wines. Besides, it's a soup (*see* Soup).

Mushrooms   Mushrooms being relatively neutral in taste, it is how and what we cook them with that will determine the wine.

Mutton   *See* Lamb.

Nachos   Lager beer or ale—not wine—is the best liquid accompaniment for this Mexican tortilla and melted cheese appetizer.

Napoleons   *See* Pastries.

Nasi Goreng   This family of Indonesian fried-rice dishes harmonizes best with lager beer or ale.

Natilla Choose a demi-sec or doux sparkling wine, letting the quality of the preparation determine the quality of the wine. A quality-matched sweet fortified wine is also in order.

Nectarine *See* Peach.

New England Boiled Dinner Rather than a wine, serve a hard cider or perhaps a lager beer or ale. If you wish a wine, consider a lightish but assertive red such as an ordinary Beaujolais.

Nuts Nuts, if not too salty, marry particularly well with most fortified wines as well as with Champagne. When they are to be eaten before dinner, serve the nuts with a dry sherry, Madeira, white Porto, or Champagne. If the nuts are consumed after the dinner, serve one of the sweeter versions of those fortified wines or Champagne. When cooking with nuts, the choice of wine will almost always be more influenced by other factors—such as cooking method, seasonings, and the other ingredients—than by the nuts per se. Keep in mind that the characters of the different nuts vary markedly. Some (pine nuts, for example) are relatively mild, while others (walnuts, for example) are much stronger in flavor and aftertaste. Some (the fresh ones) are far more delicate in flavor than those that have just begun to turn slightly rancid. Some (pistachios, for instance) vary from tame to excessively salty, depending on the processor's intent. Some (like peanuts and Brazil nuts) are not genuine nuts but are treated like nuts in cooking pots and parlance.

Octopus Your wine selection will be largely determined by the cooking method, sauce, and so forth. *See* Fish.

Oeufs à la Neige Open up your finest demi-sec or doux Champagne for this heavenly dessert. Still another option is a quality sweet fortified wine: Porto, Madeira, among others.

Oeufs en Gelée　There is simply too much egg yolk in this French first-course dish to do a wine any good. Beer is out, too, because of the dish's delicate nature. Your best bet is to forgo serving an alcoholic beverage altogether. If you have your heart set on having a wine, select a modest-priced sparkling white.

Omelet　As discussed in the Egg entry *(see)*, egg yolks can conflict with wine. If you wish to serve a wine with an omelet, don't waste a good wine.

For a plain omelet you need a fairly assertive, medium-bodied, ordinary white such as a dryish California generic Chablis or Riesling, both of which have few virtues to lose. Other make-do possibilities include a dryish rosé of good credentials or a modestly priced sparkling white wine, perhaps your best all-around choice. As you increase the butter and/or cream content of the omelet, increase the body of the wine. Similarly, as you increase the use of herbs and spices, go up the scale in terms of the assertiveness of the wine.

The characteristics of a wine needed for a filled omelet will largely depend on the stuffing or topping. If the filling is cheese, select a young, fresh, somewhat lightish and assertive red such as common Zinfandel or regional-level Côtes-du-Rhone. If the omelet is laden with a tomato, onion, and flavorful herb sauce, choose an even more robust and assertive red wine such as an average-quality Italian Chianti. With seafood fillings, choose a somewhat full yet still basic white similar to the middle-grade Muscadets and Macons. An alternative to all the above choices is a sparkling wine, with the degree of sweetness, color, and so forth being principally dependent upon the omelet filling. Still another option is to serve a lager beer, ale, or hard cider—or even a cup of coffee or tea—and forgo the wine altogether.

Onion Soup Besides being too flavorful, this French specialty is a soup, which suggests no wine (*see* Soup).

Orange This fruit, along with its citrus cousins, is too acidy for wines of any type. For a beverage accompaniment or a macerating medium, choose an orange-based liqueur, such as Grand Marnier, Cointreau, curaçao, or Triple Sec.

Osso Buco Although the Milanese braised veal-knuckle specialty is robustly seasoned, the dish is so splendid that you may be justified in opening up a medium-grade Barolo or Gattinara. More rational choices, however, would be a Valpolicella or a Bardolino. A California Grignolino is still another alternative.

Oysters Rockefeller This New Orleans–invented bacon, spinach, Pernod, and oyster specialty calls for a crisp, robust, not too costly white, such as a California Chenin Blanc or a non-*Cru* French Chablis. *Also see* Shellfish.

Oyster Stew Since it is usually creamy and well seasoned, a modest, dry, crisp wine such as a Muscadet or Macon Blanc will do. There is nothing wrong with serving a lager beer or ale either. *Also see* Shellfish.

Paella An assertive, fullish, not too expensive white such as a medium-grade Gewürztraminer or white Rioja suits this dish well, as do lager beer and ale. Some Spaniards prefer a red with this dish, but I would go along with this approach only if the Paella's principal ingredient consisted mainly or totally of items like chicken, sausage, ham, and/or pork, as opposed to seafood (yes, Paella as the Spanish know it doesn't necessarily have to have seafood—the ingredients are largely a matter of personal preference, budget, and availability).

Parmesan/Parmigiano-Reggiano An average-quality Chianti, Barbaresco, Barolo, Gattinara, or other similar medium- to full-bodied red, including an American Zinfandel from a good producer, relates well with this flavorful Italian cheese. *Also see* Cheese.

Pasta Whether it is in the shape of spaghetti, macaroni, or any other form, this durum semolina staple is basically neutral as far as wine selection is concerned. The key determinant is the sauce (though, in the case of ravioli and similar pasta creations, the stuffing also matters).

Let us first examine seafood sauces. When they are delicately seasoned, a quality, unassertive dry white like a good Soave is in order. The more the seafood sauce becomes robust with the addition of tomatoes, olive oil, onions garlic, strong herbs, and lemon juice, the coarser and less distinguished the wine should be. In either case, whether the sauce is delicate or robust, the wine should be at least medium-bodied, principally in deference to the pasta's heavy starch content.

Tomatoey meat sauces are normally assertive, acidy, and fatty, and therefore generally require a robust red that can hold its own. Opening a fine red such as the French Médocs and Côte d'Ors or even a northern Italian red such as a Barolo or Chianti Classico is a waste of money in the case of at least 90 percent of the meat sauces because the subtle nuances of those wines would probably be overwhelmed by the sauce's ingredients. Better choices would be less expensive, less superb wines, such as the ordinary Chiantis of

Italy, the Chinons and Côtes-du-Rhône-Villages of France, the lesser Riojas of Spain, and the young Zinfandels, Gamay Noirs, Petit Sirahs, and Barberas of California.

Meatless tomato sauces, including the authentic marinara, can usually be successfully combined with any of the wines just listed.

If the onions in any of the above tomatoey meat or meatless sauces are first softly sautéed, thus bringing out their natural sweet flavor, you may well choose a Lambrusco if of good background and if it possesses no more than a slight sweetness.

For sauces laden with cream, egg yolk, and/or cheese, as with Fettucini Alfredo and many other pasta dishes, you have a choice between a dry, full-bodied white (like a Hermitage or California Chardonnay) or a relatively smooth, light- to medium-bodied red (like a Valpolicella or Bardolino). Even a good Barbaresco, Gattinara, Barolo, or Chianti Classico would not be wasted and, at times, does indeed make a *bellissimo* coupling.

For mundane dishes, such as the American favorite macaroni and cheese, don't overspend—a California jug generic Burgundy is more than adequate.

If your pasta is sauced with Pesto (a personal favorite), an Orvieto works very well.

The wine for a stuffed pasta largely depends on the type of stuffing and sauce if any. Stuffed pastas, such as Tortellini, Agnolotti, Manicotti, and Cannelloni—if not seasoned with a heavy hand—call for a fine Italian red such as a Barolo or Chianti Classico. Many other stuffed pastas, such as Lasagna, are customarily well seasoned and require no more than a drinkable, robust, everyday dry red. Stuffed pastas such as Ravioli fall into no-man's-land; they can be delicately or robustly prepared, depending on the recipe.

A final note on pasta: as any good cook from Bologna

knows, pasta verde is (or should be) dyed green by soaking the freshly made dough in spinach juice. Although spinach is not on friendly terms with wine, the amount of the spinach flavor that gets infused into the pasta is so insignificant as not to be a factor in wine selection.

Pastitsio A Greek Retsina, white or rosé, or a lager beer or ale is a good choice.

Pastrami To serve a wine would be a waste. Serve a lager beer or ale.

Pastries Rich, cream-filled pastries, such as Profiteroles, Napoleons, and Mille-Feuilles, require a sweet, assertive sparkling white wine to help cut across their high fat content. A top-level sweet (demi-sec or doux) Champagne may be in order if the pastry is fresh and superbly prepared. Otherwise, serve a medium-grade white sparkling wine. More than a small amount of certain ingredients such as chocolate, however, obviate the use of a wine. A chocolate-based liqueur would thus be better for a pastry such as a chocolate éclair.

Pâté If the pâté is coarse and relatively well seasoned, like the preparation that is called country-style, choose a wine with some acid, such as the medium-grade Zinfandels, Chiantis, Chinons, and Côtes-du-Rhône-Villages—or, if you want a white, select one on the order of Rioja or Gewürztraminer. Game pâtés generally take a slightly more assertive wine than do those made from goose, pork, and calf's liver. Should you be serving the greatest of pâtés, the authentic pâté de foie gras, with or without truffles, uncork a fine brut or sec Champagne, or a fine and dryish Riesling from the Mosel or Rhine, or a fine white Côte d'Or if at least of *Pre-*

mier Cru credentials. Alternatively, as is the fading custom in Bordeaux, you may wish to serve a luscious Sauternes (but for the sake of your palate, I suggest enjoying this match-up by itself as a midday or late evening snack and not during the appetizer course of a meal, lest the sweetness of the wine diminish your enjoyment of the foods and wines that are to follow). When serving a fine wine, remember not to take even the tiniest nibble off the traditional pâté accompaniment, the cornichon—this pickle will distort your taste buds' ability to detect the delicate characteristics of the wine.

Peach One of the marriages made by the god of wine is a lusciously ripe peach (as well as a nectarine) with a glass of fine French Sauternes, ideally a Château d'Yquem of fine vintage. Sweet Champagne and sweet fortified wines (Portos, sherries, etc.) are almost—though not quite—as good a match-up. Another alternative is a peach-based liqueur.

Peach Melba Far better than any wine for this peach, ice cream, and raspberry-sauced dessert is the framboise eau-de-vie or, to a lesser extent, one of the peach-based liqueurs.

Peanut Stew Accompany this West African specialty with a good beer or ale. If you prefer a wine with this dish (I don't), stick with an inexpensive, assertive California red jug wine.

Pear To do its best with a wine, the pear must be of top quality and in a perfect state of ripeness. A sweet dessert wine such as a fine French Sauternes or a Hungarian Tokay (of five *puttonyos*) is an ideal selection. So is a Poire William brandy.

Peking Duck   The sauce is too sweet and sour, and the raw scallion is too assertive, to do any wine a good deed. Drink the Șhaohsing rice "wine," lager beer, or ale, or the Chinese white lightning named Mou-Tai.

Pecorino Romano   Partnering well with this flavorful Italian cheese are average-quality Chiantis, Barbarescos, Barolos, Gattinaras, and other similar medium- to full-bodied reds, including an American Zinfandel from a good producer. *Also see* Cheese.

Petit Suisse   Open a fullish, inexpensive red California jug wine such as a generic Burgundy for this rich, creamy French cheese. *Also see* Cheese.

Picadillo   There is too much seasoning in this dish for all but a few very ordinary robust red wines, like some of those coming out of Sicily. A lager beer or ale makes better sense.

Pickles   Any pickle—gherkins, sweet, and dill included—plays havoc with wine because of the substantial vinegar content.

Pie   Serving a wine with pie seems a little out of character, both from a culinary and from a historical point of view. This mistake is especially blatant with pies such as pumpkin, lemon meringue, and Key lime, though one wouldn't be committing an unforgivable culinary sin by serving a sweet Asti Spumante or a similar fruity medium-grade sparkling wine with a berry or stone-fruit pie if the filling is not cloyingly sweet. To minimize the effect of the pie's acidity and sweetness, garnish the dessert with a dollop of unsweetened whipped cream.

Pilaf Your best bet is a lager beer or ale, but if the pilaf is not overly seasoned, you may serve a young Beaujolais, Gewürtztraminer, or Macon Blanc, depending on the type of meats and/or vegetables used in this Middle Eastern dish.

Pineapple Though this tropical fruit is one of the most glorious-tasting produce items on earth, marrying it with a wine does each a great harm; they create negative off-flavors in each other, primarily the result of the pineapple's natural acidity. Your best match-up is a pineapple liqueur, crème d'ananas being the best known.

Pipo Crem' A great wine will surely be overpowered by this bluish-greenish veined cheese. However, you can uncork a robust yet good wine such as a medium-quality Hermitage, Côte Rôtie, or Châteauneuf-du-Pape. *Also see* Cheese.

Pizza With an infinite number of possible topping combinations, there is no single wine that can go with all pizzas. However, your best all-around choices will probably be a medium-grade Italian Chianti or California Petit Sirah, a young Zinfandel or Barbera, or a modest California jug red generic. As the use of garlic, anchovies, hot red pepper, and other wine-hostile ingredients increases, go down the quality scale when selecting a wine. Lager beer and ale are also good liquid accompaniments to pizza.

Plum A Mirabelle, Quetsch, or (the slightly firey) Slivowitz plum brandy is a smarter choice than a wine for this fruit because of the plum's acidy taste. If a wine is desired, select a sweet Champagne or perhaps a fortified wine such as a sweet sherry or Porto.

Poires Hélène The chocolate topping nixes the use of a wine. Suitable accompaniments include a pear brandy or a chocolate-based liqueur, such as Cheri-Suisse.

Pont l'Évêque Try a parish-level Côte de Nuits Burgundy (such as Nuits-Saint-Georges or Gevrey-Chambertin), Saint-Emilion, Pomerol, Hermitage, Côte Rôtie, Châteauneuf-du-Pape, California Pinot Noir, or a similar full-bodied red with this square-shaped, surface-ripened French cheese. *Also see* Cheese.

Pork As far as wine selection is concerned, the flavor of the flesh of the pig tends to be neutral, but not quite so much as is the case with chicken and veal. Thus, except for the smoked products, such as bacon and ham, the wine will largely be determined by such factors as the cooking method, the sauce, and the seasoning (*see* pages 8 to 15), not to mention the age and inherent quality of the pig and the cut of the joint.

As a general guideline (if we don't follow it too blindly), we could get along by remembering to serve a medium- or full-bodied white, or a light- or medium-bodied red with enough fruit and acidity to cut through the normally high fat content of pork. Some of the wines that more or less satisfy these criteria are Beaujolais, lighter red Côte d'Or Burgundies (such as a Santenay or Monthélie of medium-quality vintage), Valdepeñas, Côtes-du-Rhône-Villages, and certain young regional Bordeaux. On the white side, suitable wines include the Alsatian Gewürtztraminer, young German Rieslings, Vouvrays of medium-dry vintages, Macons, the medium-dry Graves, and the California Chardonnays and Johannisberg Rieslings. Nonstill table-wine choices are sparkling whites, rosés and hard cider, lager beer and ale.

You will not need to buy more than a medium-priced bottle for most pork dishes. If you use a fruit garnish or stuffing, such as pineapple, apples, or prunes, spend even less.

For specific suggestions on some two dozen pork dishes, *see* their appropriate individual entries. *Also see* Ham.

Port Salut   A Côte de Beaune (parish level), Morgon, Moulin-à-Vent Beaujolais, California Zinfandel, Mercurey, Rully, or other similar medium-bodied red combines successfully with this French cheese. *Also see* Cheese.

Porterhouse Steak   Perhaps the happiest marriage is a red Côte de Nuits from the village of Nuits-Saint-Georges, ideally one of *Premier Cru* status. A fine California Pinot Noir or Cabernet Sauvignon is also a worthy match.

Potage Saint-Germain   *See* Soup, and particularly its discussion of cream soups.

Potato Salad   The mayonnaise-dressed potato salad fares better with wine than does its vinaigrette-dressed sibling. Either way, don't waste any more than an inexpensive dry to medium-dry white or rosé wine on this popular summer preparation.

Pot-au-Feu   This dish can be made with beef or chicken, depending on the cook's desire. If with chicken, serve a medium-priced white, such as a Macon-Villages, Sancerre, or California Pinot Blanc. If beef is used, a Beaujolais-Villages, a southern red Burgundy such as a Mercurey, or a California red Gamay pairs well.

Pressed Duck   *See* Duck and Goose, Domesticated.

Prime Rib   If the meat has been simply roasted or grilled, serve one of the bigger red Côte d'Ors, such as a *Premier* or *Grand Cru* Gevrey-Chambertin.

Profiteroles   *See* Pastries.

Prosciutto and Melon (or Figs)   A fortified wine such as a dry vermouth or sherry is an infinitely better choice than a table wine for this well-known appetizer.

Provolone   Good choices for this flavorful Italian cheese include an average-quality Chianti, Barbaresco, Barolo, Gattinara, and other similar medium- to full-bodied reds, including an American Zinfandel from a good producer. *Also see* Cheese.

Quenelles de Brochet   If delicately made and sauced, open up a fine *Premier* or *Grand Cru* white Côte de Beaune, such as a Meursault or even a Montrachet. The use of a Sauce Mousseline or even a Sauce Nantua should not alter your wine choice so long as you keep them from being too rich or assertive.

Quiche   The French Alsatians and Lorrainians have more different quiches than there are days in the year; Quiche Lorraine, despite what most Americans think, is but one example of this immense variety. Since the dough encasement is basically neutral, the filling determines the wine. If the filling is loaded with egg yolks, as is the case with most quiches, including Quiche Lorraine, a good wine is wasted. Because a Quiche Lorraine also contains a fair amount of cheese and bacon, a light-bodied red with a certain degree of acid to cut across the fat is needed; a French Chinon or Bourgueil or a young California Zinfandel suffices rather well. A medium-grade dry sparkling wine also performs well. Among the still whites, the popular choices are an Alsatian Riesling and a Gewürztraminer.

Rabbit If the rabbit is young and roasted, a medium- to full-bodied white, such as a California Chardonnay, or a light-bodied red, such as a Beaujolais-Villages, are good choices. If it is in a stew or deep-fried Southern-style, choose a more robust white, such as a Macon Blanc, or a less delicate Beaujolais, one without special credentials. *Also see* Game.

Raclette While a white Swiss wine, such as one from the Valais canton, is customarily called for with this melted-by-the-fire cheese dish, a light-bodied red such as a Swiss Dole or a Côtes-du-Rhône-Villages would do the Raclette more justice. Stay away from fine wines because of the Raclette's traditional pickled onion, cornichon, and ground pepper accompaniments.

Raisins A sweet fortified wine such as a Porto, Madeira, or Marsala is your sensible choice.

Raspberries One of the world's most celestial rewards is the eau-de-vie crème de framboises. With raspberries it is heavenly, either as a macerating medium or as an accompanying beverage. For wine affinities, *see* Berries.

Ratatouille An assertive, inexpensive, dryish white, rosé, or even a red from sunny Provence (or a similar wine) is a good marriage for this French Mediterranean medley of eggplant, tomatoes, garlic, and onions, to name but four of the extensive number of possible ingredients.

Ravioli   *See* Pasta.

Reblochon   You would do well to open a parish-level Côte de Nuits Burgundy (such as Nuits-Saint-Georges or Gevrey-Chambertin), Saint-Emilion, Pomerol, Hermitage, Côte Rôtie, Châteauneuf-du-Pape, California Pinot Noir, or similar full-bodied red. *Also see* Cheese.

Rice   Like Pasta *(see)*, white rice is neutral. The wine selection will be determined by the sauce or by the dish's other ingredients, be they lamb, chicken, vegetables, herbs, or spices. Assuming that sauces and coingredients are equal, the more flavorful brown rice calls for a more assertive wine than does its sibling, the polished white rice. For specific wine match-ups for the more popular rice dishes, *see* their individual entries.

Ricotta   When used as an eating as opposed to a cooking cheese, serve a young, firm ordinary red wine such as a California mass-produced Barbera. *Also see* Cheese.

Risotto Milanese   Rather than being served by itself, this Piedmontese saffroned-rice specialty is meant to accompany a more flavorful item, such as the braised veal shank in Osso Buco. Consequently, the wine selection is determined by the dish's principal preparation. For wine selections for risotto preparations in general, *see* Rice.

Roast Beef   This name can cover a variety of cuts: prime rib, sirloin, round, and fillet, to name just four. While all require a fullish red wine, those from the tenderloin call for a top-level Côte de Nuits Burgundy or a similar wine. Good all-around choices from California include the medium to top grades of Zinfandel, Cabernet Sauvignon, and Pinot Noir.

Roast Chicken   The flavor of this oven-cooked bird is somewhat too strong for a white wine. A light- to medium-bodied red on the order of a young Zinfandel or red Loire Chinon or a Spanish Valdepeñas makes a better choice. Take into consideration the stuffing, if any; for instance, if the bird's cavity contains a well-seasoned stuffing, don't waste your money paying for subtleties in the wine.

Roast Duck à la Montmorency   *See* Duck and Goose, Domesticated.

Roast Lamb   *See* Lamb.

Roast Pork   If simply roasted, serve a light- to medium-bodied red such as a Beaujolais-Villages or perhaps a Côtes-du-Rhône-Villages. Other possibilities include a medium- to full-bodied white such as a good southern white Burgundy on the order of a Pouilly-Fuissé or one of the other better whites from the Macon district. A California Chardonnay also works well, as do sparkling wine, lager beer, and ale. Your biggest culinary concern should be to avoid the fruit garnishes and stuffings, such as prunes and apples, as they can interfere with the enjoyment of the wine.

Roe   True caviar, and I am talking about the processed roe of the sturgeon, deserves something special—and the better the quality of the caviar, the more special the wine should be. For the very best grade of caviar, such as fresh, unpasteurized Beluga Malossol, uncork your finest brut Champagne—or, as the Russians do, serve it with a fine, ice-cold vodka or other relatively flavorless white liquor. Another alternative is to serve a *Premier* or *Grand Cru* hyphenated Montrachet, Meursault, or Corton. Still another fine fish egg specialty is shad roe; with this springtime specialty serve a top-grade Alsatian Gewürtztraminer or a Loire Sancerre. With Taramasalata, the Greek roe mixture, enjoy a white or rosé, Retsina, or lager beer. For salmon roe, a medium-grade Chardonnay or a schnappslike white liquor will do. However, for the rock-caviar, such as the black-dyed lump-fish roe (which I personally detest), serve no better than an inexpensive white jug wine.

Ropa Vieja Generally, a lager beer or ale should be served with this dish.

Roquefort Being the most delicate and refined of the vari-ous blue cheeses, this ewe-milk product can be partnered with a slightly better wine than is called for by its sister cheeses, Gorgonzola and Stilton. Hence, a top-quality Her-mitage, Côte Rôtie, or Châteauneuf-du-Pape would not be out of order. *Also see* Cheese.

Rum Cake A compatible liqueur or a sweet, ordinary for-tified wine such as a Malmsey Madeira can best stand up to the strong flavor in this dessert.

Sabayon *See* Zabaglione.

Sachertorte This classic Viennese chocolate-covered cake calls for a suitable liqueur, such as a Sabra, Cheri-Suisse, Swiss Marmot, or Vandermint—or coffee, which is my first choice.

Saint-Marcellin A fine red Côte de Beaune Burgundy, such as Volnay or Pommard, complements this French goat-milk cheese. *Also see* Cheese.

Saint-Maure Follow the same advice given for Saint-Marcellin *(see)*.

Saint-Paulin Wines that combine well with this French cheese include Côte du Beaune (parish level), Morgon or Moulin-à-Vent Beaujolais, California Zinfandel, Mercurey, Rully, and other similar medium-bodied reds. *Also see* Cheese.

Salade Niçoise The recipe for this specialty varies from Provence household to household, and from day to day, depending on what's fresh and available in the local markets. If your recipe is more or less typical, thereby containing garlic, anchovies, vinaigrette dressing, tomatoes, peppers, and/or capers, I wouldn't suggest any wine save a coarse white on the order of a dry, inexpensive Provence white. If extra anchovies are put into the salad, switch to a dry fortified wine, such as a dry vermouth.

Salade Vinaigrette The acidic dressing makes wine taste sourish. For pointers on serving a salad with a meal, *see* page 23.

Salisbury Steak Nothing better than an ordinary jug red should be served with this onion-laden ground-beef patty.

Salmon Roe *See* Roe.

Saltimbocca Serve the wine used to cook this dish or serve an ordinary, not too full Chianti or a good white Soave.

Samsoe Try a fair- to good-quality Hermitage, Côte Rôtie, Châteauneuf-du-Pape, Chianti, Rioja, Zinfandel, or other similar assertive, somewhat fruity medium- or full-bodied red with this cheese. Nonwine alternatives: a quality lager beer, ale, or hard cider. *Also see* Cheese.

Sauerbraten   A good, strong German beer is by far the best choice for this chunk of meat that has been well marinated in vinegar and other strong seasonings. Of the various wines, a not too expensive Gewürtztraminer works best.

Sausages   Most sausages tend to be too well seasoned for wine. If eaten by themselves, those sausages generally do better with a lager beer or ale than with a wine. Some sausages, such as Boudin Blanc and other creamy white sausages, are more mildly seasoned, but still seasoned enough to preclude drinking a fine, delicate wine. With a sausage of the latter type I would suggest a Gewürtztraminer or any dry and robust, not too expensive white wine.

Schnitzel à la Holstein   Essentially, this is a Wiener Schnitzel *(see)* topped with a fried egg and usually anchovies, both of which are hostile to wine. Consequently, a lager beer or ale is your best selection.

Scotch Woodcock   The anchovy ingredient argues against serving a wine with this scrambled eggs on toast specialty.

Scungilli   If this food is served with a hot sauce (which is typical), drink a lager beer or ale. When scungilli is the star of a vinegar-sauced salad, an inexpensive but assertive white jug wine is also a good companion.

Senegalese Soup   This creation is far too spicy to benefit any wine. Enjoy it solo.

Shad Roe   *See* Roe.

Shark's Fin Soup A dry *Shaohsing* Chinese rice "wine," or a dry fortified wine such as a sherry would be adequate, but I strongly contend that this distinguished Chinese specialty is better off on its own.

Shell/Delmonico Steak Select a quality red Côte de Nuits Burgundy or, from California, a medium- to top-grade Cabernet Sauvignon, Pinot Noir, or Zinfandel.

Shellfish Since shellfish are even more delicately flavored than fish, the wine selection determinants, such as the cooking method and sauce, discussed under Fish *(see)* apply even more here. Shellfish are subdivided into two major categories: mollusks (including oysters, clams, mussels, scallops, abalone, scungilli, cockles, whelks, and periwinkles) and crustaceans (lobsters, shrimps, crabs, crayfish, prawns, and scampi, among others).

Mollusks, if plainly cooked, tend to need a crisp, bone-dry wine, while the crustaceans get along better with a slightly fuller and not so bone-dry wine. Thus, for mollusks plainly prepared or served on the half shell, wines such as Chablis (the classic affinity with oysters), Muscadet, Gros Plant, and Verdicchio are ideal. For plainly prepared crustaceans, a dry medium-bodied wine, such as good parish-level Côte d'Or or Graves, or a better than average California Chardonnay would be in order. Champagne goes with either, but naturally the mollusks would demand brut.

As a shellfish grows in size, it tends to lose its delicate flavor and texture, as you can readily perceive by cross-tasting a littleneck, cherrystone, and chowder clam (all three, for the record, are the identical species—they are just at different growth stages).

I know it's traditional and zestfully rewarding to sprinkle lemon on shellfish, but do so niggardly—or not at all—if you plan to serve a fine wine. The same self-denial goes for other popular shellfish perkers: Worcestershire, Tabasco, chili, and similar assertive sauces. Should you prefer those piquant seasonings, drink an ordinary everyday wine or—even better—a lager beer or ale.

Oysters have a more delicate flavor than clams, which are in turn more delicate than mussels. Therefore, you can open a better wine for oysters, perhaps a *Grand Cru* Chablis of good vintage. But keep in mind that all things called oysters are not alike, as there are different subspecies, living environments, and so forth, creating different flavors and textures.

The last of the four most popular mollusks, scallops, are slightly sweeter in flavor than oysters, clams, and mussels. Consequently, a medium-dry wine would not be out of order. This is especially true for bay scallops, which are sweeter as well as more tender than the large sea scallops.

Some crustaceans are more delicate and have just a hint more natural sweetness than do others. Of the three most popular crustaceans, lobster is the most delicately flavored and textured as well as the sweetest. Next comes the crab, followed, in last place, by the shrimp.

As with the mollusks, crustaceans differ among their own species. Among the lobsters, for instance, the Maine variety is perceptibly better than the spiny lobster. As far as those lobster tails are concerned, they are relatively coarse, usually frozen, and are not even lobsters in the first place, as they are, more often than not, the rear ends of large South African or Australian crayfish. The same misnomer goes for virtually all "scampi" sold in American restaurants, including the "gourmet" Italian ones. These so-called scampi are in reality jumbo shrimp, a far cry from the true scampi of the northern Adriatic Sea, which is significantly sweeter, more tender, better flavored, and finer textured. In the crab family, some—like the blue crab—are infinitely better tasting than the Alaskan king crab. So, take into consideration those quality variables when making your wine selection.

Freshwater crayfish can be very delicately flavored, but much depends on the flavor of the water they live in, which can be influenced by man or nature or both. If they come from the comparatively pure streams of northern Scandinavia, these crayfish can be exceptional. Traditionally they are served with a vodka or similar white liquor followed by a beer chaser, as in Finland, but a wine such as a good Swiss Neuchâtel makes a worthy substitute.

Shepherd's Pie   Serve an English beer or ale with this meat pie.

Shish Kebab   Having been marinated and well seasoned, this specialty calls for a red wine such as a Spanish Valdepeñas, a French Beaujolais, or a red Gamay from California. Lager beer or ale also goes well.

Shrimp Cocktail   This popular American appetizer is much too spicy and tomatoey for all but a dry fortified wine or a jug-quality white wine. *Also see* Shellfish.

Shrimp Creole   Lager beer or ale are my first choices. If a wine is desired, serve an assertive ordinary white such as a modest Gewürtztraminer. A dry sherry or Madeira is still another option. *Also see* Shellfish.

Shrimp Scampi   An Orvieto does nicely if the dish is not too spiced. If so, switch to a lager beer or ale—or, if possible, a dry sherry or Madeira. *Also see* Shellfish.

Shrimp Toast   A dry fortified wine such as a Madeira or sherry or a Chinese rice "wine" is a compatible choice. *Also see* Shellfish.

Sirloin   A full-bodied red Côte de Nuits Burgundy such as a *Premier Cru*-level Fixin or one of the better Gevrey-Chambertins goes well with this beef cut. A fine California Cabernet Sauvignon marries well too.

Smoked Cheese   Select a lager beer or ale rather than a wine. *Also see* Cheese.

Snails   If served with garlic butter, as is the case usually (Escargots à la Bourguignonne, etc.), I suggest a modest, assertive white wine such as a regional-level Macon or California Colombard.

Snails à la Bourguignonne   *See* Snails.

Soft-Shelled Crabs   Pouilly-Fumé, Sancerre, and the white Hermitage go well with this late springtime and early summer favorite. *Also see* Shellfish.

Sole à la Meunière/Amandine (etc.)   *See* Fish.

Sopa de Ajo   This Spanish specialty has two strikes against it as far as an accompanying wine is concerned: It is a soup (*see* Soup), and it reeks with garlic.

Soufflé, Cheese   Serve a light, lively red such as a Beaujolais or California Gamay Noir, but do not exceed an average quality level in deference to the souffle's egg yolk content.

Soufflé, Chocolate   Nix on wines because of the heavy use of chocolate. A chocolate-based liqueur, such as a Vandermint, Sabra, or Cheri-Suisse, would be more suitable for this dessert dish.

Soufflé, Seafood   Open a medium-bodied wine with enough character to stand up to the soufflé, but delicate enough to pay homage to the seafood; a white Aloxe-Corton Burgundy or a top-grade Macon-Villages or California Chardonnay, among other similar wines, would serve this purpose. The subtleties possessed by a better wine—such as a Heitz Chardonnay—would be lost because of the marked use of egg yolks in the soufflé.

Soup   Wine imbibing and soup sipping seldom marry well, principally because there is little textural contrast between the two liquids. However, when a soup approaches or becomes a stew (like the fish concoctions such as Bouillabaisse), a wine is not out of place. A wine can be excellent with a thin soup, providing you add it to the soup instead of drinking it. If you do desire to serve a glass of wine with such a soup, try to serve the same wine that went into the soup, normally a dry fortified wine such as a sherry or Madeira. When incorporating this wine into your soup, add it at the last second, as some of the sought-after aromas of these fortified wines can quickly dissipate into the air. Whatever wine you use, buy the very best and don't use more than a minute portion lest your soup smack excessively of the fortified wine, a case tantamount to the proverbial tail wagging the dog. Thick, creamy soups, such as seafood bisques, New England clam chowder, and the various cream of vegetable soups, do little for a glass of wine, and vice versa. Each fares best by itself. If a wine is desired, I again suggest a dry fortified wine, including a dry vermouth, which is strong enough to stand up to the soup's demanding ingredients, including the cream.

Southern Fried Chicken A Macon-Villages or a medium-grade California Chardonnay fare well with this dish if well made and thus not greasy.

Souvlakia/Giro The fattiness of the lamb suggests the obvious ethnic match-up, the Greek Retsina, or Kokkineli, the red Retsina. Lager beer and ale work well too.

Spaghetti *See* Pasta.

Spinach and Mushroom Salad The acidy dressing as well as the spinach will create an unpleasant off-taste in any table wine, even the least delicate ones. A dry vermouth or perhaps a dry sherry will do if a wine is desired.

Squab *See* Game.

Squid The cooking method, sauce, and so forth are the primary wine selection determinants. *See* Fish.

Steak au Poivre No matter how good the steak may be, the excessive use of crushed peppercorns makes this specialty unsuitable for any good wine. Choose a young California Zinfandel or commonplace Chianti. Another alternative is a lager beer or ale.

Steak Diane This meat being so strongly flambéed with brandy, I wouldn't suggest anything but an assertive, not too expensive red, such as a young California Zinfandel or medium-priced Spanish Rioja. The French Côtes-du-Rhône-Villages is another option.

Steak Tartare This spiced-up chopped-beef specialty needs a robust, medium-priced wine such as an ordinary Chianti or Rioja, both of which are sufficiently assertive. However, a lager beer or ale would probably fare better.

Stilton The classic affinity (so the English tell us) is a vintage Porto. However, in reality, this bluish-greenish veined cheese is too strong for such a distinguished fortified wine. A better selection is a robust, medium-quality red wine such as a Hermitage, Côte Rôtie, or Châteauneuf-du-Pape. *Also see* Cheese.

Stracciatella *See* Soup.

Strawberries A strawberry liqueur, such as crème de fraises, is compatible, either as a drink or as a macerating medium. *Also see* Berries.

Strawberry Shortcake A sweet, assertive, and fruity sparkling wine, such as certain Asti Spumantes, goes with this famous American dessert. Also consider a strawberry liqueur.

Strudel A medium-grade sparkling white wine is a suitable choice. If this dessert is apple strudel, consider serving a Calvados or, if none is available, an Applejack brandy.

Stuffed Eggs The egg yolk and mayonnaise content of this appetizer are not exactly on good terms with wine. If one is served, choose a dry, inexpensive sparkling white with enough body to stand up to the preparation's oily character.

Stuffed Meats (in general) Stuffings for beef, veal, pork, chicken, and so forth tend to be well seasoned, and therefore a fine wine would be wasted in most instances. When having a stuffed meat dish, choose a wine with a degree of assertiveness that matches the degree of seasoning. For instance, stuffing laden with garlic and onions probably needs one of the more assertive wines, such as an Italian Barbera, a French Côtes-du-Rhône, or a young California Zinfandel.

Suckling Pig The happiest marriage is a good Champagne, preferably brut—or sec if you baste the animal with a slightly sweet liquid. The younger the pig and the better the cooking job, the finer your Champagne can be.

Suimono *See* Soup.

Sukiyaki A lager beer, ale, or sake is a better match than wine for this Japanese dish.

Suppli al Telephono A firm wine—such as a young red Rioja or Zinfandel—goes well with this stringy Italian rice and mozzarella cheese specialty.

Sushi/Sashimi Three good choices are a lager beer or ale, a sake, and a good Alsatian Gewürztraminer. You may also enjoy sipping an aquavitlike white liquor with these two Japanese raw fish specialties.

Swedish Meatballs Lager beer or ale is the best choice, though a Beaujolais-Villages, a California Gamay, or a similar wine will do in a pinch.

Sweet and Sour Pork Though no wine is perfectly adaptable to this Chinese specialty, a medium-grade demi-sec sparkling wine is your best option if you insist upon a wine. A better choice, however, would be *Shaohsing*, the Chinese rice "wine." Lager beer or ale is also suitable.

Sweetbreads A superb white Burgundy of *Premier* or *Grand Cru* class is an ideal choice if the sweetbreads are served in a rich, creamy sauce, as is the popular custom. If they are braised with a red wine, a fruity Beaujolais of good standing is a wise option.

Swiss Cheese If the cheese is American produced, a red California generic Burgundy will do. If Swiss produced, a fair-to good-quality Hermitage, Côte Rôtie, Châteauneuf-du-Pape, Chianti, Rioja, Zinfandel, or other similar assertive, somewhat fruity medium- to full-bodied red pairs well with this cheese. Best national match-up: the red Swiss Dole. Nonwine alternatives: a quality lager beer, ale, or hard cider. *Also see* Cheese.

Swiss Steak A suitable choice is a Côtes-du-Rhône-Villages or perhaps a red Swiss Dole.

Szechuan Cuisine *See* Hot and Spicy Dishes; Chinese Cuisine.

Taleggio Serve with this northern Italian cheese a Barolo, Gattinara, Chianti Classico, Chianti, Brunello di Montalcino, Barbaresco, or a similar full-bodied red. *Also see* Cheese.

Tamales A lager beer or ale makes the most pleasant choice.

Tangerine A member of the citrus family, this fruit fares poorly with wine. A wiser choice of alcoholic beverage, whether your intention is to drink it or to macerate with it, is Manderine, the tangerine-based liqueur.

Taramasalata *See* Roe.

T-Bone Steak You won't go wrong with a good red Côte de Nuits Burgundy on the order of a *Premier Cru*-level Nuits-Saint-Georges. A good domestic alternative is a top-grade Zinfandel.

Tempura A medium-grade California Chardonnay or a lager beer, ale, or sake teams well with this Japanese deep-fried yet delicate specialty.

Teriyaki This marinated broiled Japanese treat, whether made with meat or fish, harmonizes better with a sake, lager beer, or ale than a wine.

Terrines *See* Pâté.

Thousand-Year-Old Egg Aside from its egg yolk content, this Chinese specialty is too pungent to do wine anything but absolute calamity.

Tilsiter This flavorful cheese is better matched with a quality lager beer, ale, or hard cider than with a wine. *Also see* Cheese.

Tomme de Savoie A Morgon or Moulin-à-Vent Beaujolais, a medium-quality California Zinfandel, and similar medium-bodied reds pleasantly agree with this French mountain cheese. *Also see* Cheese.

Tortellini in Brodo This Bolognese specialty is self-contained with liquid, starch, and meat. A wine would serve no purpose except to get in the way of enjoying this soup cum wrapped-meat dumplings. *Also see* Soup.

Tostada Serve lager beer or ale.

Tournedos Henri IV   Because of the artichoke garnish and the Béarnaise sauce, I wouldn't waste a delicate wine on this dish. A medium-grade Châteauneuf-du-Pape is about the best wine you could intelligently serve.

Tournedos Rossini   The pâté de foie gras ingredient and the Madeira sauce preclude choosing a delicate wine. A good Hermitage or Côte Rotie serves this filet mignon preparation well.

Tripes à la Mode de Caen   A Pouilly-Fumé or Sancerre do well with this dish, but if tomatoes are used, switch to a red Loire, such as a Chinon or Bourgueil.

Triple Crème   A fullish red California jug wine such as the generic Burgundies suits this family of rich, creamy French cheeses. *Also see* Cheese.

Truffles   Since only a few inhabitants of our planet eat the costly white or black truffles by themselves, it is what these delicate fungi are prepared with that will determine the wine selection.

Truite au Bleu   *See* Fish.

Turkey   This is a strange bird as far as wine selection is concerned. The white breast meat may suggest a medium- to full-bodied white wine, while the dark meat from the leg shouts for a light- to medium-bodied red. In most cases, you will find the red to be the slightly better compromise choice.

Suitable red wine selections for a plainly roasted turkey include the better Beaujolais, California Zinfandels, Valpolicellas; the Côte de Beaune Burgundies such as a parish-level Volnay; the better Rhônes, such as Châteauneuf-du-Pape; the superior red Loires, such as a Chinon. Other workable choices include the medium-level classified grades of Médoc, Saint-Emilion, and Pomerol from Bordeaux.

Worthy white wine choices include the Côte de Beaune, such as Meursault; the better Macons, Graves, and Hermitages; the sound Alsatian Gewürtztraminers; the dryish Rieslings of the Rhine; and the California Chardonnays and Johannisberg Rieslings.

Besides the above red and white table wines, consider a brut or sec Champagne, which, I think, is an ideal companion to turkey.

When stuffing your turkey, be careful about adding too much of those well-seasoned ingredients, such as sausages. Also be chary about fruit garnishes. Should you serve your turkey in this manner, choose a coarser and less expensive wine than you would if the turkey were delicately prepared.

A Thanksgiving dinner poses a special problem. The bird is traditionally accompanied by cranberry sauce, an enemy of wine. Your best course of action is either to serve a wine of no more than common credentials, to eat only token bites of the cranberry sauce and subsequently cleanse your palate with a piece of bread, or to forgo the cranberry sauce altogether. The latter alternative is the wisest path to follow. With a Thanksgiving dinner, incidentally, the best wine seems to be a brut or sec Champagne, because it can foil and stand up to the dinner's heavy sauces and ingredients as well as add a little sparkle to this happy family festivity.

Tybo Pairing well with this cheese is a fair- to good-quality Hermitage, Côte Rôtie, Châteauneuf-du-Pape, Chianti, Rioja, Zinfandel, or other similar assertive, somewhat fruity medium- or full-bodied red. Nonwine alternatives: a quality lager beer, ale, or hard cider. *Also see* Cheese.

Valençay A fine red Côte de Beaune Burgundy such as a Volnay or Pommard goes well with this French goat-milk cheese. *Also see* Cheese.

Veal Veal being basically a neutral meat, your choice of wine for veal will largely depend on factors such as the cooking method, the sauce, and the seasoning (*see* pages 8 to 15). However, there is an additional consideration that particularly applies to veal: You will notice a distinct flavor and textural difference between the young milk-fed veal popular in France and Italy and the grain- or grass-fed veal typically sold in America. The latter type of veal is coarser in texture, less delicate in flavor, and in most instances should be classified as baby beef, that awkward "teen-ager" period the bovine is in between its better-tasting childhood and adulthood states. Thus, American-style veal calls for a lesser quality, more robust wine than does its European counterpart (though some of the latter can be found in ethnic markets such as those patronized by immigrant or first-generation Italian Americans).

Should you wish a very sweeping guideline for selecting a wine to go with veal, you will be generally (but not always) safe by selecting a medium- or full-bodied white, a light- to medium-bodied red, a rosé, or a sparkling wine. Whatever the wine classification, your veal dish will probably call for a dry or perhaps a medium-dry wine. Unless the sauce or seasoning is very assertive, the wine should not be too assertive lest it overwhelm the delicate veal meat. Finally, white-sauced veal generally calls for a white wine, while the brown-sauced or tomato-enriched examples are usually partnered with a red wine.

You will find specific wine selections for various veal dishes in the individual entries in this encyclopedia.

Veal Birds Usually the stuffing is too well seasoned for anything but a modest, somewhat robust white on the order of a Macon Blanc or a medium-grade California Sauvignon. If a red wine is desired, select a Valpolicella or Bardolino.

Veal Chops If the chops are simply sautéed with butter, with the possible addition of cream to the sauce, serve a full-bodied white on the order of a top-grade California Chardonnay or a white Hermitage. If the sauce is spiked with a brandy or fortified wine, stick with the same wines, but go down a rung in quality.

Veal Cordon Bleu A white Spanish Rioja, a California Sauvignon, or a French Beaujolais-Villages are three good choices for this veal, ham, and cheese concoction.

Veal à la Française A very good white Côte d'Or Burgundy (Chassagne-Montrachet, Meursault, etc.), up to and including the *Grand Cru* level, or a superb California Chardonnay makes an ideal companion for this dish, which happens to be one of the most delicately prepared of the veal scallopini preparations.

Veal Marsala You need a reasonably assertive wine, such as an Orvieto or a dry Sicilian white, to stand up to the Marsala in this dish. Serving that Italian fortified wine, Marsala, if dry, is not a bad idea either.

Veal Milanese Follow the same suggestions mentioned for its culinary sibling, Wiener Schnitzel *(see)*. However, since Veal Milanese customarily uses a butter rather than a lard cooking medium, you are justified in going up the wine-quality scale a notch or two; hence, you might select a superb example of a French Chinon. Another possibility is a Valpolicella or Bardolino—or, from California, a young, not too full Zinfandel.

Veal Orloff The Mornay and Soubise sauces incorporated into this elaborate veal creation argue for a light-bodied red with some acidity, such as a young Zinfandel or red Loire. A regional-level red Bordeaux is another possibility. Any finer wine would be wasted, notwithstanding this dish's high reputation among nineteenth-century gourmets.

Veal Parmigiana Choose an everyday robust wine, perhaps a California jug generic Burgundy or the like, for this spicy Neapolitan specialty. One of the drier Sicilian reds is not a bad choice either, nor is lager beer or ale.

Veal Piccata Not too fine a wine should be used for this dish because of its lemony character, but a wine such as a white Orvieto or Macon Blanc, or a red Bardolino or Valpolicella would be suitable.

Veal Roast A Beaujolais-Villages (and if this dish is well prepared, even a Moulin-à-Vent or Morgon) makes pleasant culinary music with this dish. On the white-wine side, think of a California Sauvignon.

Veal Scallopini/Escalopes The wine for this thin, pounded piece of meat can vary, depending upon what the chef has done to the veal scallopini. For instance, he could make Saltimbocca, Schnitzel à la Holstein, Veal Birds, Veal Cordon Bleu, Veal à la Française, Veal Marsala, Veal Milanese, Veal Parmigiana, Veal Piccata, Vitello Tonnato, Wiener Schnitzel (for specific wine suggestions for these famous preparations, *see* their individual entries).

Vegetables In most meals a vegetable serves as an accompanying dish, playing second fiddle to the main preparation. Consequently, when selecting a wine, one normally bases one's decision upon the starring entrée. This strategy is sound, providing that you don't neglect to take the accompanying vegetables into consideration, because some can interfere with the maximum enjoyment of the wine. This interference can be caused by the vegetable's intrinsic nature, by its condition and age (generally speaking, the younger and fresher a vegetable, the milder it will be), by how it was prepared (overcooking, for example, usually brings out less than desirable flavors), and by its coingredients, including the seasoning and the sauce. How much of the vegetable preparation you consume also matters, as does the manner in which you eat it; a nibble of a neutral piece of bread or of the main entreé before sipping your wine helps mend any damage to your palate.

Popular vegetables that are the worst culprits as far as delicate wines are concerned include artichokes, bell peppers, brussels sprouts, cabbage, cucumbers, endive, fennel and celeriac, garlic and other members of the onion family, parsnips, rutabagas and turnips, spinach, sweet potatoes and yams, and those "fruit-vegetables," the tomatoes. But before putting any of these vegetables on your forbidden list, take into account both the variables listed in the preceding paragraph and the quality and type of the wine you're trying to protect. Also consider drinking an assertive wine such as an Alsatian Gewürztraminer, a dry fortified wine such as a sherry, or even a lager beer or ale (providing, of course, that these alcoholic beverages are also compatible with the other preparations being served with the vegetable).

On the positive end of the spectrum are potatoes, rice, green peas, snow peas, and flageolet beans. Almost as compatible are carrots, cauliflower, and green beans—if young and fresh.

In the middle ground are a number of vegetables, among which is asparagus. While this early springtime treat is reasonably delicate, it tends to change the taste of wine (for instance, making it seem slightly sweeter than it really is). Of course, if the asparagus (or any vegetable) is served vinaigrette style, I would suggest that you forget about all but the most ordinary table wines—and probably even those. If the vegetable vinaigrette dish (asparagus, artichokes, etc.) is to be served as the main entrée, such as for a light lunch, a dry vermouth or sherry are two sound selections.

Venison   *See* Game.

Vichyssoise   *See* Soup, and particularly the discussion on cream soups.

Vitello Tonnato   The mayonnaise and tuna in the sauce of this heavenly warm-weather Milanese specialty complicates our wine selection decision, but the anchovies and the ample use of lemon juice make our task even more difficult. I would suggest a somewhat fullish, somewhat robust white, such as a good Gewürtztraminer.

Waldorf Salad   While no wine is ideal for this popular mayonnaise-dressed salad comprising apples, walnuts, and celery on top of a bed of lettuce, an inexpensive, not too sweet rosé is an adequate choice.

Welsh Rarebit/Rabbit   Since this contains both beer and mustard, a lager beer or ale—but never a wine—is your best liquid companion to this famous Welsh specialty.

Wensleydale   A better alternative to wine for this English cheese is a lager beer, ale, or hard cider. Exceptions to this rule include the vintage Portos. *Also see* Cheese.

Wiener Schnitzel Ideally, you should have a red that is both light-bodied (in deference to the veal) and somewhat acidy (to cut through the cooking-fat residue). Meeting this set of criteria are, among others, a red Loire, such as a Chinon, and a young, not too expensive California Zinfandel. A traditional alternative is a fresh, dryish Austrian white, such as Rhine Riesling, but I think that match-up was created more as a result of geographical availability than for reasons of natural affinity. Also, instead of wine, think in terms of a lager beer or ale.

Wild Rice The wine for this precious American Indian grain will be determined by the meal's other dishes, but wild rice's lack of delicate flavor precludes serving a wine with too much finesse and subtlety.

Won Ton Soup Savor this Chinese soup by itself, without liquid accompaniment. *Also see* Soup.

Yakitori A lager beer or ale, sake, or a modest sparkling white pairs well with this marinated chicken preparation of Japan.

Yang Chow Fried Rice Since anything can go into this peasant dish, designed to use up leftovers, it is hard to pinpoint a specific wine. Curiously, the authentic Chinese version, which employs no soy sauce, is better suited for a wine than the soy-sauce-drenched Chinese-American version. Whatever wine you choose, make it robust and inexpensive lest this dish overwhelm the wine's subtle nuances. All in all, usually your best choice is a beer or a dryish *Shaohsing*, the so-called Chinese rice "wine" (it is really more of a beer than a wine).

Yankee Pot Roast Yankee and most other pot roasts, such as Boeuf à la Mode, can get by with an ordinary California Pinot Noir, a top-grade Petit Sirah, or a similar medium-bodied red wine.

Zabaglione The best and most logical accompaniment is the same sweet fortified wine you used to concoct this frothy egg yolk, sugar, and Marsala creation.

Zarzuela de Mariscos *See* Fish.

Zuppa alla Pavese Not only does the fact that this northern Italian specialty is a soup argue against serving a wine (*see* Soup), but the whole raw egg that is dropped into the bowl doesn't exactly befriend a wine.

Zuppa Inglese Think in terms of a compatible liqueur or a sweet fortified wine such as a Marsala for this Italian rum-soaked sponge and custard cake, curiously named "English soup."

IV
Mini-Guide to Wines

As any experienced wine drinker knows, it is difficult to describe in words the characteristics of a particular wine. Within any given wine category, there is simply too much variation in flavor and bouquet, among other factors. For instance, some Bordeaux wines bear more resemblance to certain Burgundy wines than they do to their Bordeaux kin. Also, some wines, such as the Zinfandels, cover such a broad spectrum of characteristics that the name Zinfandel by itself gives you only a vague indication of what you will find in the bottle.

Yet, despite the above restrictions, some description is better than none for the person just beginning to learn about wines. For the benefit of those of you who fall within this neophyte category, I've prepared this mini-guide to some of the more popular wines (sorry, with over five thousand wines in the world, I could not cover all of them). Please keep in mind that many exceptions to the rules exist and that this mini-guide is only meant to give you general guidelines.

Bardolino   Red wine from northern Italy near Verona. Slightly lighter bodied and colored than Valpolicella, which it slightly resembles. Best when drunk under three years old. Made from a variety of grapes.

Barolo   Red Italian wine from Piedmont. Dry, full-bodied. Robust and with some fruitiness when young—needs long maturing to develop finesse. Made from the Nebbiolo grape.

Beaujolais   French dry red (plus an inconsequential amount of white, which resembles the neighboring southern Macon). Most of the reds (made from the Gamay grape) are light- to medium-bodied, fresh, fruity, short-lived, with a slight spicy accent. Some reds—especially Moulin-à-Vent and Morgon—are fuller, less fruity, and longer lived—more like a southern Côte de Beaune wine than what one thinks of in terms of the characteristic Beaujolais. For the latter, the Fleurie is perhaps the finest, most respected example. Other countries produce pseudo-Beaujolais wines, but these are only Beaujolais in name, not in character.

Bordeaux   The four best known red-wine-producing districts are the Haut-Médoc, Saint-Emilion, Pomerol, and Graves. The best of the Haut-Médocs (Châteaux Lafite-Rothschild, Mouton-Rothschild, Margaux, and Latour) are the most delicate, elegant wines in the world. Those from the Saint-Emilion and Pomerol districts are fuller and more robust, somewhat in the style of a Côte de Nuits Burgundy. Those from Graves somewhat resemble the Haut-Médoc, though the average-quality level is not as good. The best known white-wine-growing districts are Graves (primarily dry white) and Sauternes (luscious, sweet dessert wines).

Burgundy (American) This is a generic wine, meaning that a winery can use any grape, the only unofficial restriction being that the color of the wine be the traditional red. While the products vary considerably from winery to winery, they always lack finesse. They are, in a phrase, merely ordinary day-to-day drinking wines that should be enjoyed, not discussed.

Burgundy (France) The finest portion of the Burgundy wine region is the Côte d'Or, which is further subdivided into two parts: Côte de Nuits in the north and Côte de Beaune in the south. Côte de Nuits is celebrated for producing the world's best full-bodied reds—Chambertin and Romane-Conti being two celestial examples. The Côte de Beaune, on the other hand, is noted for producing the world's most superb dry white wines, such as the great Montrachet. Its reds are generally softer than those from the Côte de Nuits, though the Corton is certainly an exception to that rule of thumb.

Cabernet Sauvignon A red, dry, varietal wine. Principal U.S. source: California. The inexpensive wines display almost every characteristic except that of Cabernet Sauvignon. The better made Cabernet Sauvignons are full-bodied, with a complex bouquet and flavor—and with excessive tannin unless allowed to age at least approximately five (often ten) years.

Chablis The authentic Chablis of France is a crisp, dry white wine. Body ranges from medium- to full-bodied (the better ones are on the fuller side). The pseudo-Chablis made in America and other non-French lands is generic, meaning that it can be almost anything the producer wants it to be (but not having nature on its side, the producer can never make it taste like the true Chablis).

Chardonnay Dry, white varietal wine. Principal U.S. source: California. Also called Pinot Chardonnay. Most examples are medium-bodied, with pleasant fruit. Better Chardonnays are full-bodied, with an unmistakable soft, elegant power.

Châteauneuf-du-Pape Red and white from France's Rhone Valley. Red is dry, high in alcohol, full-bodied, with powerful bouquet and some fruit—it needs aging to soften the edges. White is full-bodied and somewhat assertive, yet with pleasing roundness.

Chenin Blanc Dry white varietal wine. Princpal U.S. source: California. Medium-bodied, flowery, with some robustness.

Chianti Dry red from the Tuscany region of Italy. Fruity, vigorous, with firm bite. Medium to full body. Most Chianti is common and should be drunk young. Some Chianti, on the other hand, can be superb with a great complexity. One way to find the best is to look for Chianti Classico, easily identified by the black-rooster insignia on the neck of the bottle. This latter wine should be aged at least five, sometimes ten, years. Made from several grapes, the principal one being Sangiovese.

Côte Rôtie Red from France's Rhône Valley. Full-bodied with powerful, generous bouquet and obvious fruit. Needs maturing. Made from various grapes.

Côtes-du-Rhône Red and white from France's Rhône Valley. Red is dry, medium-bodied, without the depth and complexity of the Rhône's best wines (Hermitage, Côte Rôtie, etc.), but is generally a good value. White is dry, medium-bodied, and generally a notch or two below the red on the quality scale.

Gewürztraminer Dry white French wine from Alsace. Has a spicy taste, making it ideal for certain well-seasoned foods. Most of the wine is medium-bodied.

Hermitage Red and white from France's Rhone Valley. Red is dry, full-bodied, with intense bouquet with noticeable fruit—needs years of aging to develop properly. White is dry, full-bodied, with sophisticated assertiveness.

Macon Dry white (some red) French wines made in the Macon area, in southern Burgundy. It is made from the Chardonnay grape and is generally dry and medium-bodied, though some of the better examples, such as Pouilly-Fuissé, can be noticeably fuller.

Mosel This is the French counterpart of the Rhine Riesling, both being made from the same grape. On the average, Moselles are drier than their German Mosel counterparts, making the Moselles generally more suitable as a dinner wine.

Muscadet Dry (often crisp) white French wine from the lower Loire Valley. It is usually medium-bodied, with charactertistic acidity. The best comes from the subarea officially called Muscadet de Sèvre-et-Maine (look for that name on the label).

Petit Sirah   A dry red California varietal wine. Typically, it is robust, somewhat tannic, nothing to rave about, medium- to full-bodied. Yet the short-in-supply better versions have most of the crude corners rounded off, giving the knowledgeable drinker an earthy wine worth enjoying.

Pinot Noir   Dry red varietal. Principal U.S. source: California. Medium- to full-bodied. The best can have a big and complex flavor and bouquet but certainly not in the same league as with the best of France's Côte d'Or Burgundies, which are produced exclusively from the Pinot Noir grape.

Pouilly-Fuissé   *See* Macon.

Pouilly-Fumé   Dry white French wine from the upper Loire Valley. Medium-bodied with a distinctive, somewhat assertive flavor, but if from a better year and vineyard, the wine gets fuller.

Rhine   The best wines in Germany come from the Rheingau, an area producing white wines exlcusively from the Riesling grape. Most of this flowery wine is within the medium-bodied range. The degree of sweetness is broad, from slightly dry to lusciously sweet, as is the case with the fabled Trockenbeerenauslese.

Riesling (American)   Dry white varietal. Johannisberg (or White) Riesling is the true Riesling of Rhine and Mosel fame. It does well in California, producing a dry, crisp, medium- to full-bodied white with good fruit. Of mere ordinary credentials are the Emerald Riesling (a cross between the Riesling and a lesser grape) and the Grey Riesling (without a single drop of the Riesling in it).

Rioja   Dry red and white from Spain. The red is generally medium-bodied, robust with tannin, firm fruit, and woody taste, the result of relatively long aging in the barrel. There is a big difference in quality between the average and the top-of-the-line Riojas. The white is medium-bodied, somewhat assertive. Both red and white are made from several grapes.

Soave   Dry white wine from northern Italy near the town of Verona. It can be light- to medium-bodied (the fuller the wine, the better the Soave tends to be).

Valpolicella   Ruby-red wine from northern Italy near the Romeo and Juliet city of Verona. It is medium-bodied and has medium alcoholic strength, fruit, and some assertiveness. Best when drunk under four years old. Made from a variety of grapes.

Verdicchio   Dry (often crisp) white wine from central Italy. Medium-bodied, though some of the inferior versions are a bit thin.

Zinfandel   Red California varietal wine. Characteristics vary enormously, depending on producer, year, and so forth. It can be, for instance, a young, medium-bodied, fresh, and fruity wine with that ineffable "Zinfandel berry" bouquet, or, on the other extreme, a big, full-bodied, mature wine with more class but with less fruit and freshness.

Index